Folk Guitar

for beginners

Alfred, the leader in educational publishing, and the National Guitar Workshop, one of America's finest guitar schools, have joined forces to bring you the best, most progressive educational tools possible. We hope you will enjoy this book and encourage you to look for other fine products from Alfred and the National Guitar Workshop.

An Easy Beginning Method

PAUL HOWARD

Acquisition, editorial: Nathaniel Gunod, Workshop Arts
Internal design: Cathy Bolduc,Workshop Arts
Music typesetting: Joe Bouchard, Workshop Arts
Photo acquisition: Michael Allain, Workshop Arts
CD recorded at Bar None Studios, Cheshire, CT
Cover illustration: Jennifer Jessee

Contents

A compact disc is available for this book. This disc can make learning the examples in this book easier and more enjoyable. The symbol above will appear at the beginning of every example or song.

Use the CD to make sure that you are capturing the feel of the examples, interpreting the rhythms correctly, and so on.

The track number below the symbol corresponds directly to the example or song you want to hear. Track 1 will help you tune to the CD.

Have fun!

About the Author

Paul Howard has been a guitar instructor and performer for over twenty years. His experience includes rock, county, folk and jazz styles on both acoustic and electric guitar. He began private teaching in 1970 and graduated with honors from Central Connecticut State University in 1972. Paul has been a faculty member at the National Guitar Summer Workshop since its inception in 1984. He also operates his own music school in Avon, Connecticut. Paul released two albums with his band, Last Fair Deal, and can be seen playing around New England with the Paul Howard Group. He also tours nationally with the Stacy Phillips/ Paul Howard Duo.

Introduction

Congratulations. You are about to join a large and distinguished group of people, from all walks of life and all cultures, who enjoy playing folk music on the guitar. They accompany themselves singing and in many cases take their performing to a high art.

The general definition of "folk music" is music that it is handed down from generation to generation, or person to person, by ear, by rote and imitation. There is no substitute for listening to performers, both on recordings and in person, to learn the subtleties of any style. This book is an attempt to pass along essential information that will help you in your listening and learning. Hopefully, it will clear up some of the mysteries you may encounter.

This book deals with North American folk guitar styles. There are many other beautiful folk styles from South America, the British Isles and many other ethnic traditions and nationalities. Although they are beyond the scope of this book, they should definitely be on your list of music to hear.

Learning to use the chords and techniques in this book creatively and imaginatively will bring you hours of joy. It will also point you in the right direction as you begin your journey of discovery into the world of folk music and guitar. This book is mostly concerned with using the guitar as an accompaniment instrument for singing. The melodies of all the songs are written out in standard notation (see appendix). The guitar parts are only written in tablature, so a knowledge of standard music notation is not necessary.

As you begin to learn the songs and techniques in the book, try to apply this information to the thousands of other songs you can learn from other song collections and friends. Check around your town or city for other people interested in folk music, and you may find a thriving "scene" you hadn't noticed before. Community bulletin boards, local newspapers, folk radio and the internet are all sources to network with other like-minded folks.

Have a great journey!

Many great singers and players have traveled this road before you. Here are some players you may want to get acquainted with:

Big Bill Broonzy
Joan Baez
Greg Brown
The Carter Family
Elizabeth Cotton
Rev. Gary Davis
Ani DiFranco
Bob Dylan
Woody Guthrie
Mississippi John Hurt
Lonnie Johnson
Robert Johnson
Patty Larkin
Leadbelly
Brownie McGhee
Joni Mitchell
Odetta
John Prine
Jimmie Rogers
Bill Staines
James Taylor
Merle Travis
Josh White
Muddy Waters
and many more.

Chapter 1

Getting Started

Parts of the Guitar

The biggest part of the guitar is the body or sound box. The neck extends out to the headstock. The front of the neck is the fingerboard which contains the frets. The strings are suspended between the bridge and the nut. When you strike a string without pressing down on a fret it is called an open string.

The pitch (highness or lowness) of the string is changed by pressing down immediately behind one of the frets with a left-hand fingertip so that the string comes in contact with the fret. This creates a new vibrating string length, and thus a different pitch. The further towards the body you go, the shorter the vibrating string length and the higher the pitch.

The strings are connected to the tuning machines on the headstock and secured at the bridge by the bridge pins, tail piece or tie-ons depending on the type of guitar. Most folk guitarists use a steel-string acoustic guitar (flat-top) or in some cases a nylon-string (classical) guitar. The steel-string will be a bit more versatile for playing the music in this book. It is also louder and better for flat-pick style playing.

The sound hole allows the sound box to project tones that have been produced by the vibrating strings and the resulting movement of the wood of the guitar. It is a good idea not to let your arm come across and press on the face of the guitar and deaden the vibrations of the top. Let it ring, baby!

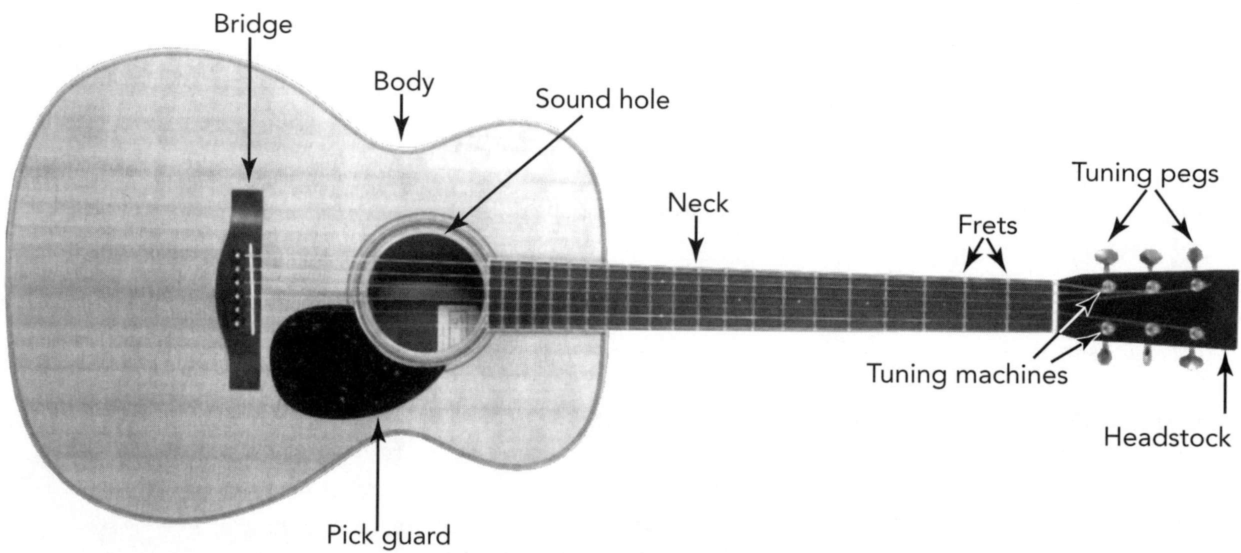

Holding the Guitar and Basic Techniques

Sitting and Standing

Now that you know which end is up, the next step is to get comfortable holding the guitar. The pictures at the right will help you understand the positions.

Most players prefer to sit with the guitar body balanced on the right leg with the right forearm gently resting on the top edge of the instrument. You must learn to balance the guitar without any support from either hand. Your hands will have enough other work to do. If you are left-handed and playing a lefty-strung guitar, you can reverse all of these instructions, although many left-handed people play the guitar in the way described here.

If you stand, use a strap and don't let the guitar hang too low. Have a repairman install a strap button near the heel of the neck so you won't have to tie the strap at the headstock. This is more comfortable and provides better balance.

Basic Techniques

This book will discuss both fingerstyle and pick-style playing. In some cases the examples can be played either way. Try some of these techniques on the open strings of the guitar.

Flat-Picking

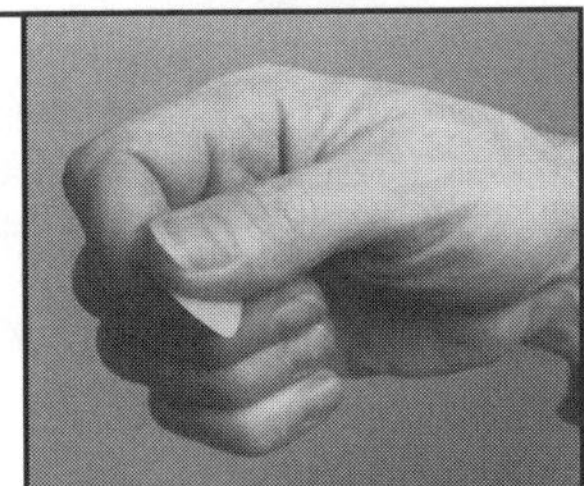

When you use a flat pick, grip it between your right-hand thumb and index finger in a firm yet relaxed manner. Avoid excess tension in your hands. Let the pointed edge of the pick protrude from the side of your thumb like a flag.

Fingerstyle

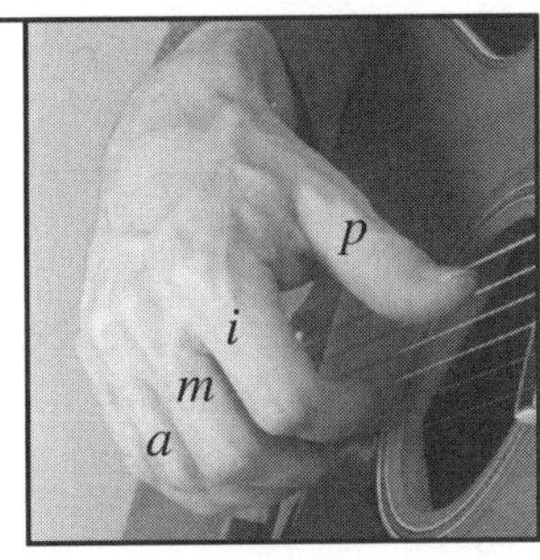

To get your right hand positioned correctly for fingerstyle, rest your forearm, just below the elbow, on the edge of the guitar. Let your hand loosely hang down to the strings with your fingers slightly curved as if holding an egg. Extend your thumb (move it away from your palm) so that it is more or less parallel to the strings and strike the lowest (6th) string with the outside edge of your thumb. Use a little flesh and a little nail moving the thumb from the wrist joint (where the thumb connects to your wrist), not the tip joint (the last joint before the nail). Note the names of the right-hand fingers: *p* (thumb) *i* (index) *m* (middle) and *a* (ring).

Strumming

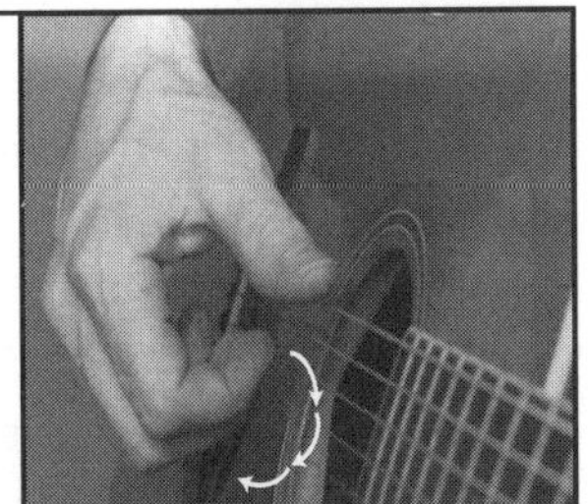

One of the strumming options from the fingerstyle position is to strum downward across the strings with the back of your fingernails by extending your fingers away from your palm. Make it more of a finger motion than a hand motion.

Left Hand

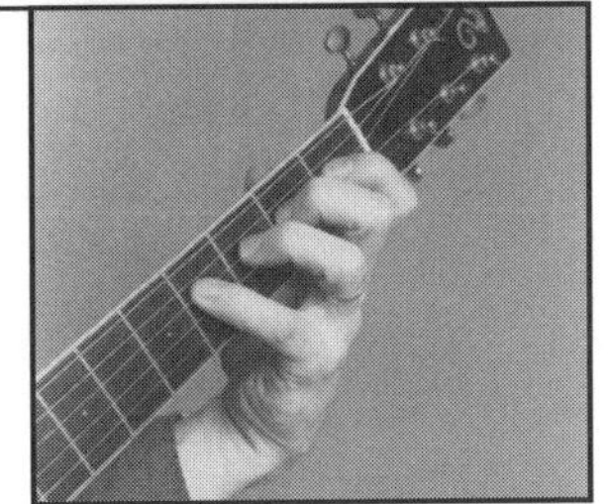

When using your left hand to fret notes, keep your thumb behind the neck. Keep your wrist low toward the floor. Stay on your finger tips and place them directly behind (to the left of) the frets. Press just firmly enough to make the notes sing and arch your fingers. Avoid excess tension.

Tuning the Guitar

Learning to tune is one of your first chores as a guitarist. While you may not have a refined enough ear to hear the relative highness and lowness of pitches yet, you will find that your ear, and your ability to tune, will develop rapidly.

Using a Keyboard

There are many ways to go about tuning the guitar. If you have a piano or keyboard, the diagram below will show you which notes match the correct pitch for each open string. Strike the piano note first, then strike the guitar string and turn the appropriate guitar tuning peg to tighten the string to bring it up to pitch, or loosen the string to bring it down to pitch. Repeat the process for each string. You could tune to another (in-tune) guitar in the same manner.

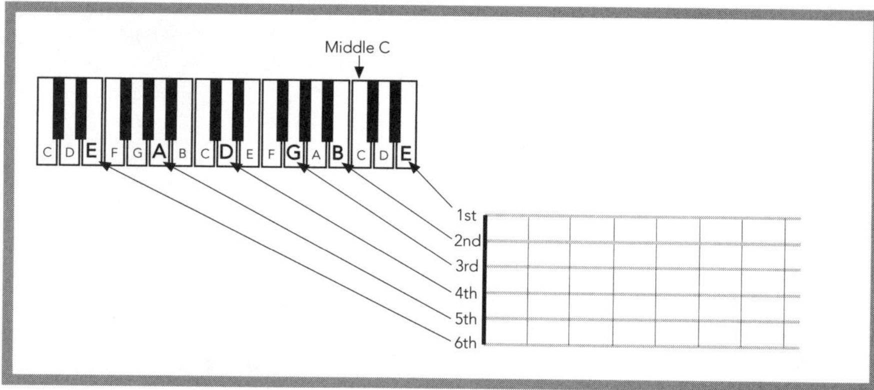

Electronic Tuners

An electronic tuner can be used to tune your instrument. They run from $20 to more than $80 depending on the features. The tuner has a microphone that picks up the sound of a string when you strike it. If you have an acoustic/electric guitar you can plug it in. Some tuners will have a read-out that tells you what note the pitch is close to, and then a meter or lights show when the note is in tune. Some tuners have a switch you must turn to select the string you are tuning. Always strike the note firmly, make your reading and tune.

Relative Tuning

Another method of tuning is to compare notes on adjacent strings of the guitar. This is called relative tuning, because they will be in tune relative to each other. Most notes can be played in more than one place on the guitar. This allows us to compare the sound of two notes which should be identical. Study the diagram on the right and you will see that note on the 5th fret of the 6th string will give you the pitch for the open 5th string. This relationship exists between all the pairs of strings except the 3rd and 2nd strings; play the 4th fret of the 3rd string to get the pitch for the 2nd string. If you tune this way, you may not be in tune with other instruments, but the guitar will be in tune with itself. Be careful that the pitch of the 6th string is not too high. If it is, some of the higher strings could break because of the extra tension.

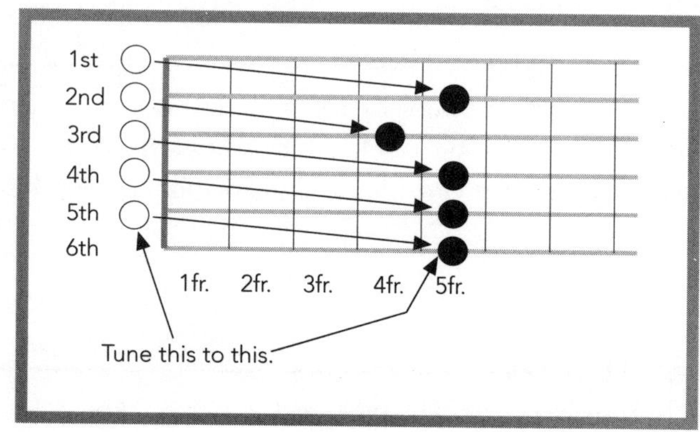

Reading the Examples in this Book

Even though folk music is basically an oral tradition, in order to write a book such as this, some form of notation is needed. This page will help you get started. For more information, see the appendix on page 46.

Tablature

All guitar music will be presented in a form called TAB (tablature). This system of notation has been used in one form or another since the Renaissance period (1450-1600) when it was used commonly for lute and guitar music. The six lines of the TAB represent the six strings of the guitar. The lowest line represents the low 6th string. Numbers written on the lines represent frets to play. An "0" indicates an open string. In this TAB system, stems and beams on the notes will show the note values (duration) of each note. Note values are measured in beats. A beat is the basic pulse behind the music—you are marking beats when you tap your foot to music. Note that chord strums and notes played by the right-hand thumb (*p*) are stemmed down. This causes certain notes to have two stems, which makes it easy to read the rhythms and identify thumb-notes.

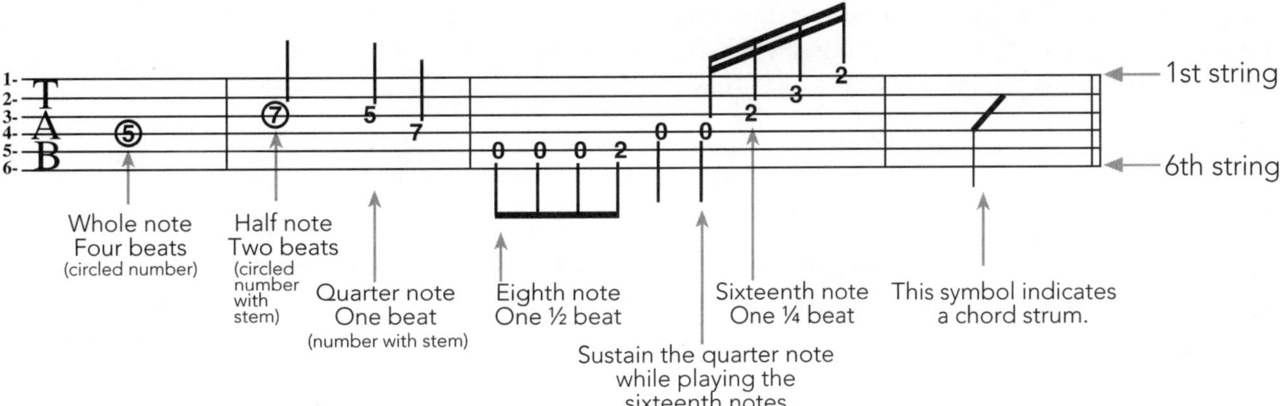

Chords

Chords will be shown by means of the standard guitar chord diagram. The chord name is shown under the diagram.

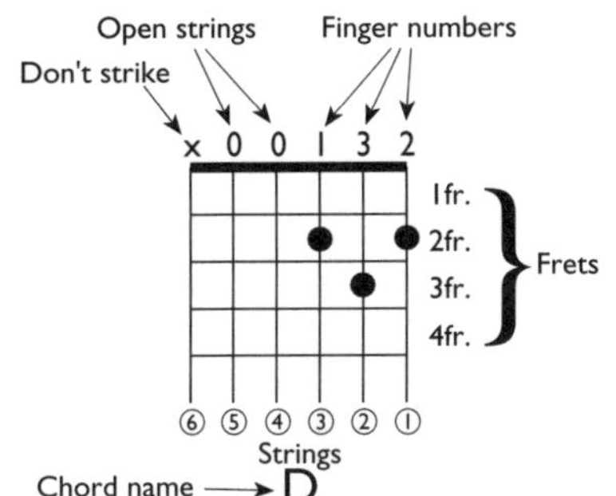

The TAB is divided into equal groups of beats called measures by means of vertical barlines. Numbers at the beginning of the TAB tell us how many beats are counted in each measure. This is called the *time signature*. The most common time signature is $\frac{4}{4}$, which means to count four beats per measure. A double bar shows the end of a song.

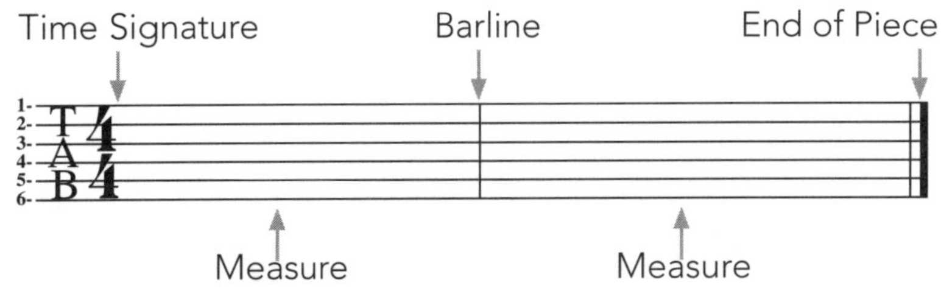

Melodies

The vocal melodies to the songs will be shown in gray standard music notation. This will allow you to learn the melodies to unfamiliar songs. There is an appendix at the back of the book (page 46) that discusses the basics of standard notation.

All Together Now

When all of these notational forms are used together, the music will look like the example on the right. Notice that one verse of the lyrics is included. The rest of the lyrics for all the songs can be found on the inside front and back covers.

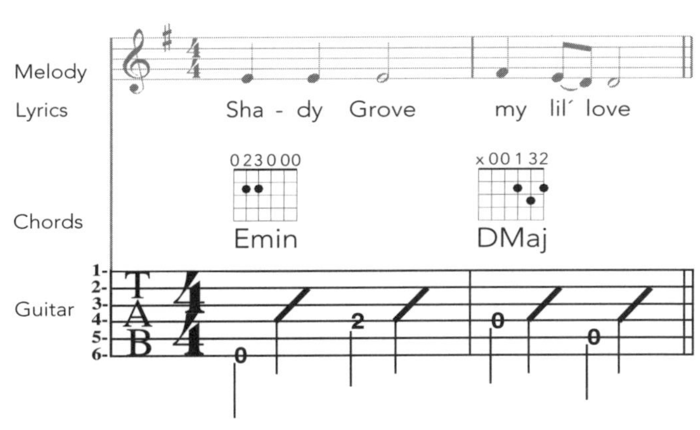

Chapter 2

Let's Make Some Music

Warm-Up

We will begin with a simple exercise. It will get both hands working. Practice slowly and work for a good, clear tone on each note. Be conscious of keeping the beat steady as you play. Rhythm is the basis of all music, so start now to keep good time.

If you are using a pick, hold it as described on page 5 and pick downward, towards the floor. Remember to stay relaxed. If you are plucking (fingerstyle) with your right hand fingers, alternate your index (*i*) and middle (*m*) fingers. Strike the string with an upward motion toward the palm of your hand, keeping your hand still. Use the corner of your finger and combine a little flesh and a little nail. See page 16 for more about fingerstyle technique. Keep your left hand in good position as described on page 5. Press with your fingertips, directly behind the frets. Arch your fingers!

Here's the exercise:

- Play the open first string.
- Play the 1st-fret note with the 1st finger.
- Play the 2nd-fret note with the 2nd finger.
- Play the 3rd-fret note with the 3rd finger.
- Repeat this process.
- Now do the same exercise twice on the 2nd string.
- Continue in this manner on the remaining four strings.

> *Important Tips*
> *Keep each finger depressing its note as you add the other fingers. This will help you develop finger independence and a smoother sound. Keep your left hand wrist and thumb positioned correctly so you can reach all the frets, especially as you get to the lower strings. Keep your hand still—let your fingers do the work.*

1

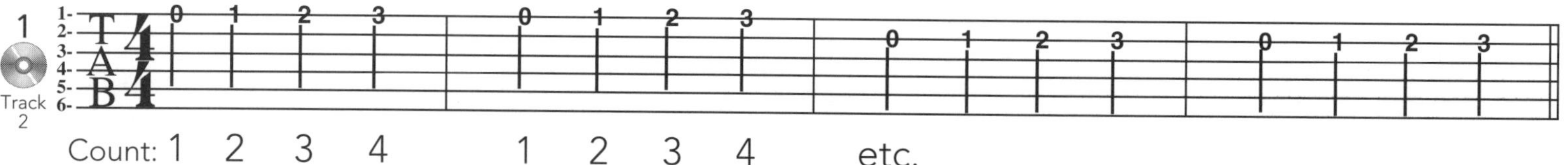

Count: 1 2 3 4 1 2 3 4 etc.

Four-String Chords

It's time to try your first *chords*. A chord is any group of three or more notes played together, so they are produced by striking three or more strings at a time. We will start off with the simple four-string chords shown on the right. These will get your fingers used to arching and staying out of the way of adjacent strings as you fret the necessary notes. Notice that in each chord, some of the notes are open strings. While holding down the proper frets, try striking the top four strings one at a time. Make sure all the notes are ringing out. Now, try to strum downward over the four stings together using a pick, the back of your nails, or even your thumb. Make it a light, quick motion so that all four strings sound almost simultaneously.

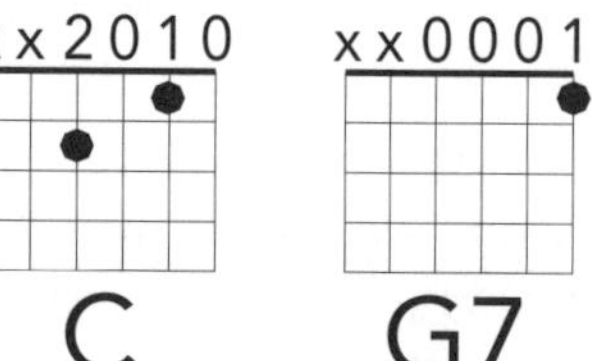

Try the following examples keeping a slow, even beat as you change from chord to chord. Strum once for each slash mark (/).Notice the repeat signs at the end of each example (the double bar with two dots). This means to return to the beginning and play again. After the second time through, just strum the first chord once to create a nice ending.

2 Chords

Track 3

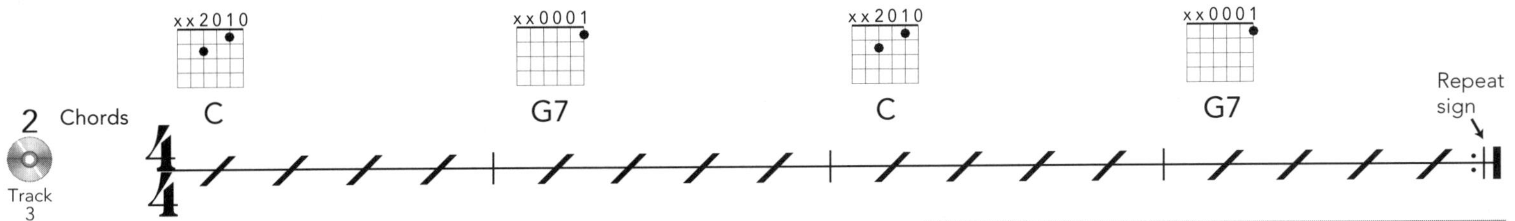

Repeat signs indicate that the music between them should be played again. If the whole song or example is being repeated, only the right repeat sign is needed.

Now try singing *Skip to My Lou* while strumming the chords as indicated. Strum once for each beat. Keep strumming through melody notes that are held for more than a beat. The accompaniment has its own steady rhythm. It is a good idea to strum two measures of chords before singing.

Notice the M.M. = 90 marking at the beginning of this song. This is a metronome marking. A metronome is an adjustable device that indicates the exact tempo (speed) of a piece. This is a great tool to have. Just set the metronome to 90, and strum once for each clicking sound, and you'll be ready to go.

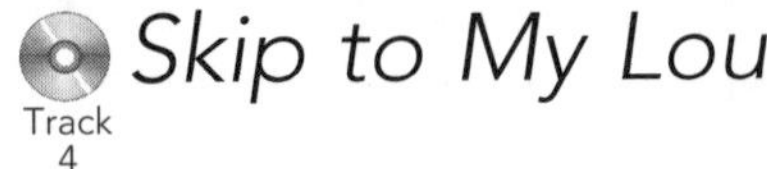

Skip to My Lou

Track 4

Traditional

M.M. = 90

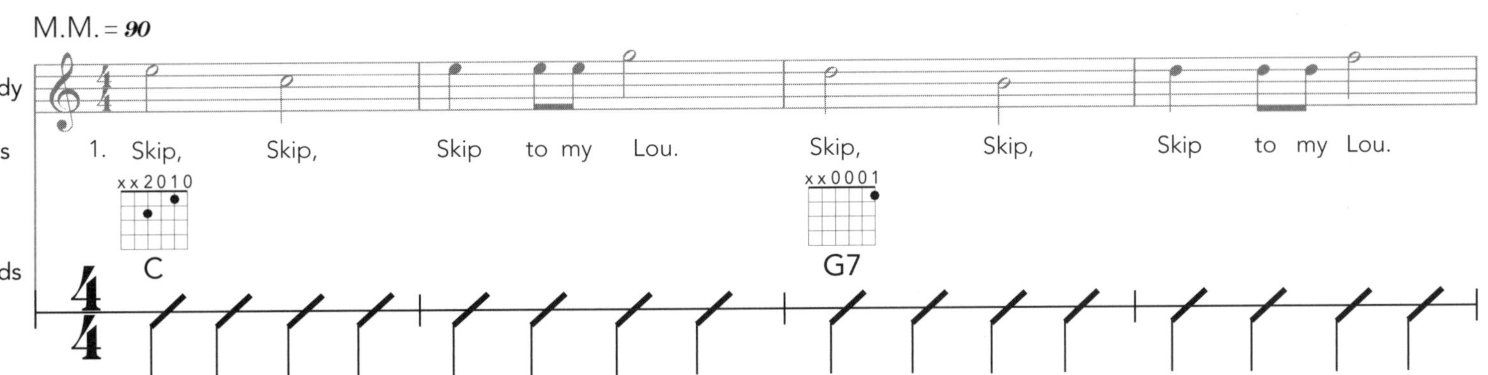

Full Chords & Bass/Strum Accompaniments

There are three basic types of chords: major, minor and dominant 7.

Chord type	Written	Sample
Major	note name	C =C Major
Minor	min	Emin = E Minor
Dominant 7	7	A7 = A Dominant7

You are probably eager to learn some chords that make use of the lower strings of the guitar and have a fuller sound. One of the easiest full chords is E Minor:

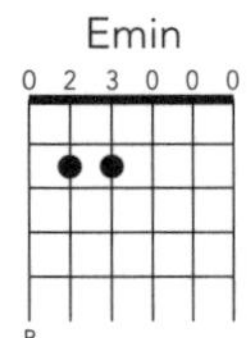

Try singing *Hey, Ho, Nobody Home* while strumming the full six-string Emin chord, once for each beat. Keep it steady!

Hey, Ho, Nobody Home

Track 5

M.M. = 96

Traditional

Now let's learn two more important chords, D and A7. From now on, as you learn new chords, you should learn where the main bass notes fall in the chords. The bass notes are low notes that are often struck as single notes within a chord. They can be used as part of a rhythm pattern. The diagrams show the main, root bass notes (R) for D and A7. The root is the note that gives the chord it's name. For instance, "E" is the root of an E Minor chord.

Try playing Example 3; hit the bass note with your pick or thumb followed by a chord strum with your pick or the back of your nails. Don't re-strike the bass note when you strum.

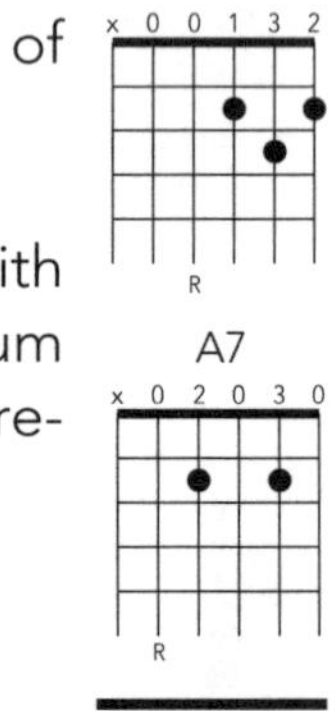

3 Track 6

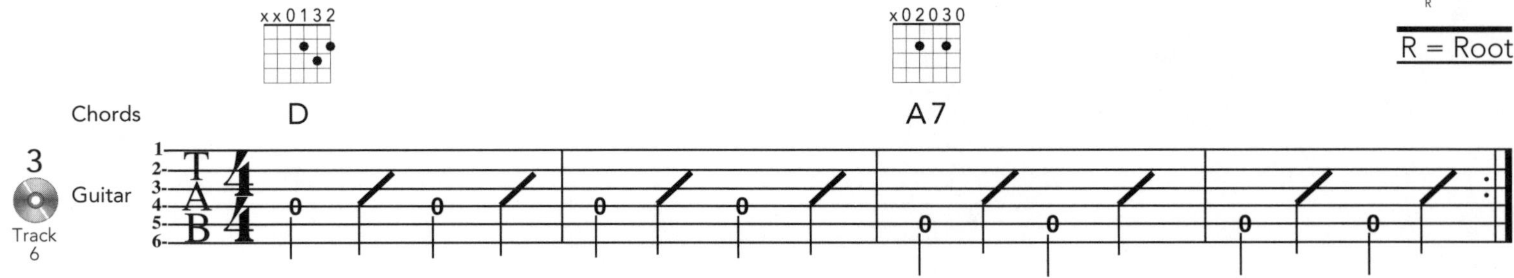

Now lets learn the full G Major chord and its bass note. The next example combines it with E Minor.

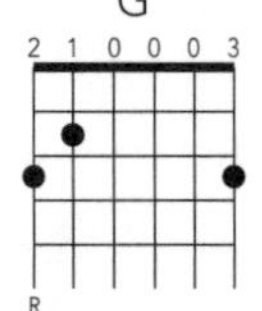

If the stretch is too difficult, use the four-string G7 until can finger the G chord comfortably.

4 Track 7

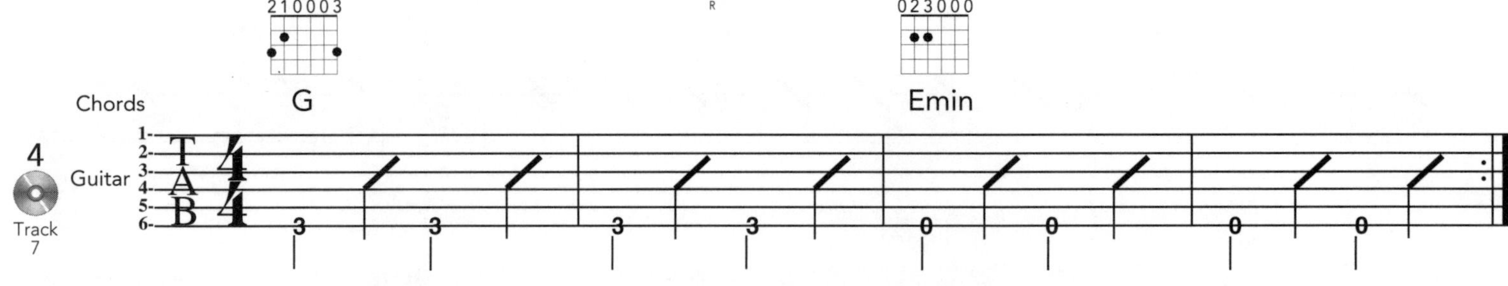

Here are two songs using this basic bass/strum accompaniment. Take your time and have fun!

> *The first note in this song is a pickup note, which is a note that occurs before the first full measure. Count 1, 2, 3 and begin playing on 4.*

Remember, you can find the rest of the lyrics for these songs on the inside front and back covers.

Swing Lo', Sweet Chariot

Track 9

M.M. = 116

Traditional

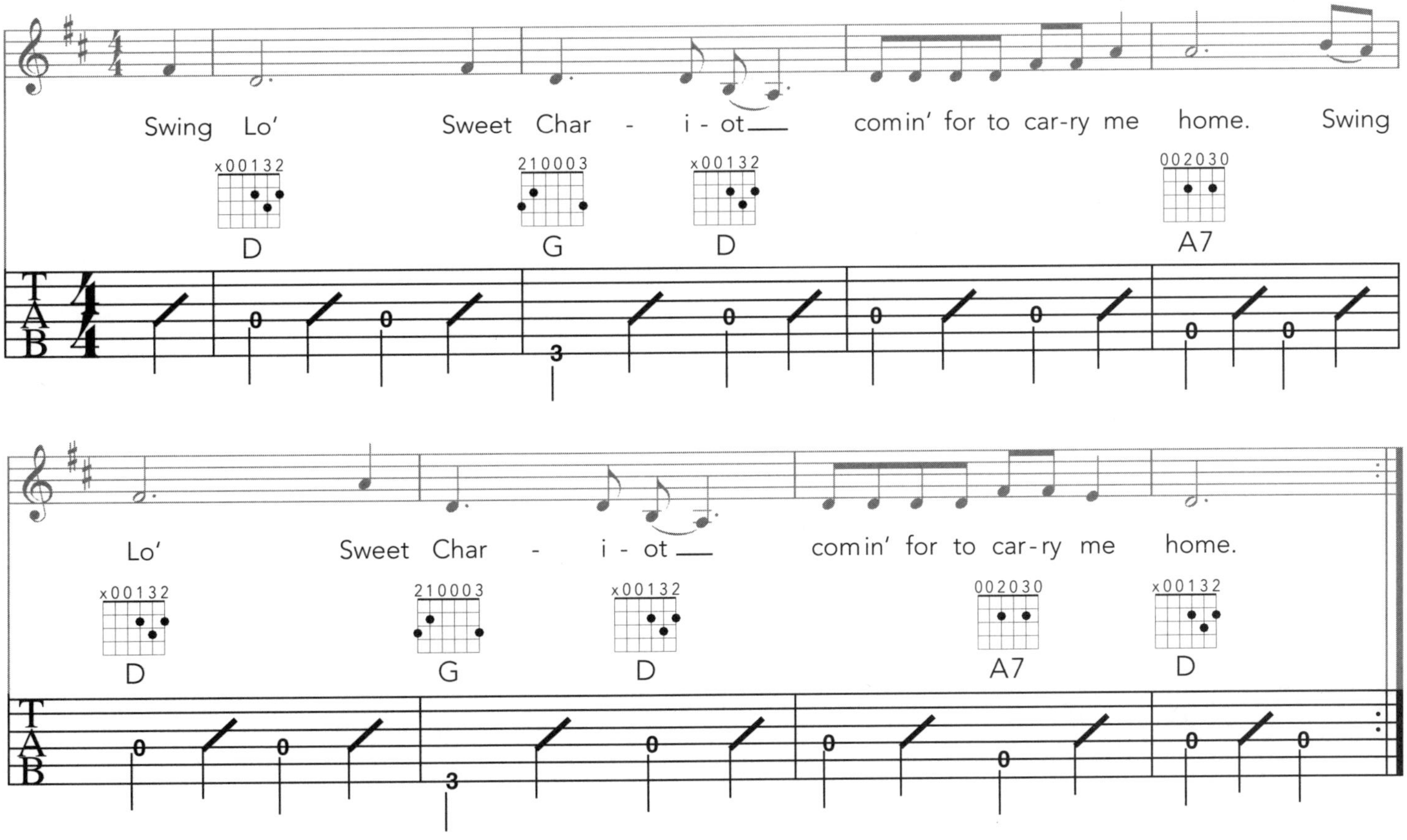

Swing Lo' Sweet Char - i - ot__ comin' for to car-ry me home. Swing

x00132 D — 210003 G — x00132 D — 002030 A7

T A B: 0 0 | 3 0 | 0 0 | 0 0

Lo' Sweet Char - i - ot__ comin' for to car-ry me home.

x00132 D — 210003 G — x00132 D — 002030 A7 — x00132 D

T A B: 0 0 | 3 0 | 0 0 | 0 0

Chapter 3

More Chords and the Capo

Primary Chords

Chords are usually played in standard combinations with other chords. These chords revolve around one basic, home-base chord, and comprise what is known as a key. The chord group used in the previous songs is D-G-A7. These are the *primary chords* in the key of D. The D chord is the *tonic* in the key of D, and is indicated with a Roman numeral **I** (1). The other primary chords are derived in the following way: Using the musical alphabet (A, B, C, D, E, F, G), count up five from the tonic (D=1, E=2, F=3, G=4, A=5). The fourth chord, G, indicated with a Roman numeral **IV** (4), and the fifth chord, A, indicated with a Roman numeral **V** (5), are the other two primary chords in the key of D.

This is true for all keys. Even better, many, many folk songs have only primary chords! That means that with the few chords you have already learned, you can literally play thousands of songs as long as you play them all in the same key.

Capo

You may have found that the pitch of the melody in the previous songs was too high or too low to sing. One solution to this problem, without learning to play in every key, is to use a *capo*. A capo is a device which clamps around the neck of the guitar and presses a rubber pad behind a particular fret. There are many different types of capos, from simple elastic models to more elegant designs. You can place the capo at any fret you wish, and then play the chords you know as if the capo were the nut of the guitar. Now the pitch of these chords will be higher. Try placing the capo up a few frets, and play the songs you've learned again to see if it is easier to sing in the new key.

Alternating Bass Notes

As you get better at the bass-chord strum you learned on page 10, you can add variety to the bass part by alternating the bass notes that you play. There are other bass notes in the chord besides the root note. These are referred to as the 5th and 3rd of the chord. They get their names by counting up five through the musical alphabet from the root of the chord. For instance, in a G chord:

G=1 (root), A=2, B=3, C=4, D=5.

In a D chord, A is the 5th. In a G chord, B is the 3rd and D is the 5th.

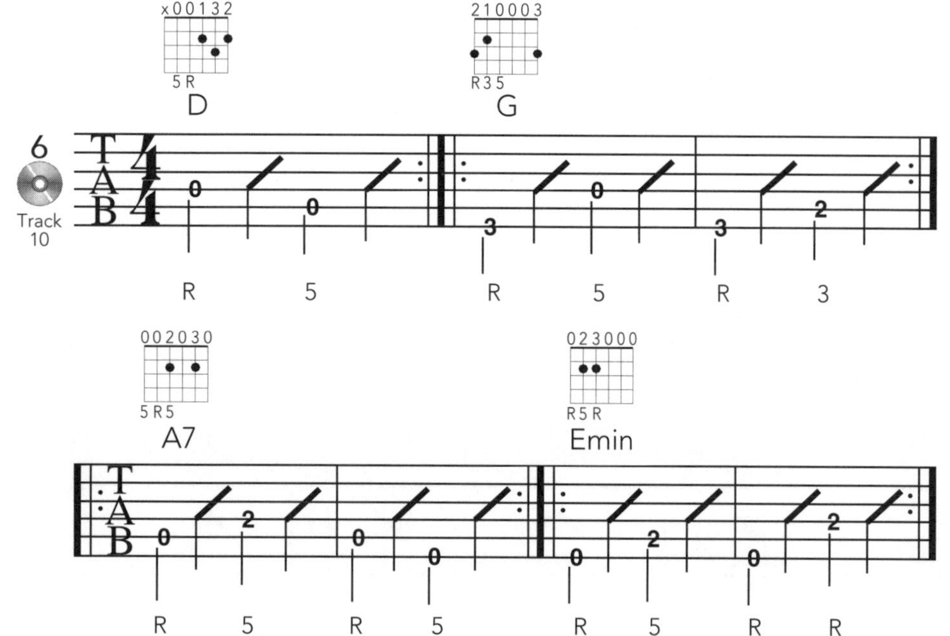

R = Root
3 = 3rd
5 = 5th

Note that both bass notes and chord strums are stemmed down.

Learn where the roots, 3rds and 5ths fall in the chords you have learned. We usually alternate between the root and either the 5th or the 3rd. Try the examples on the left, and then the arrangement of *Shady Grove* on page 13, using alternating bass notes.

Shady Grove

Track 11

Traditional

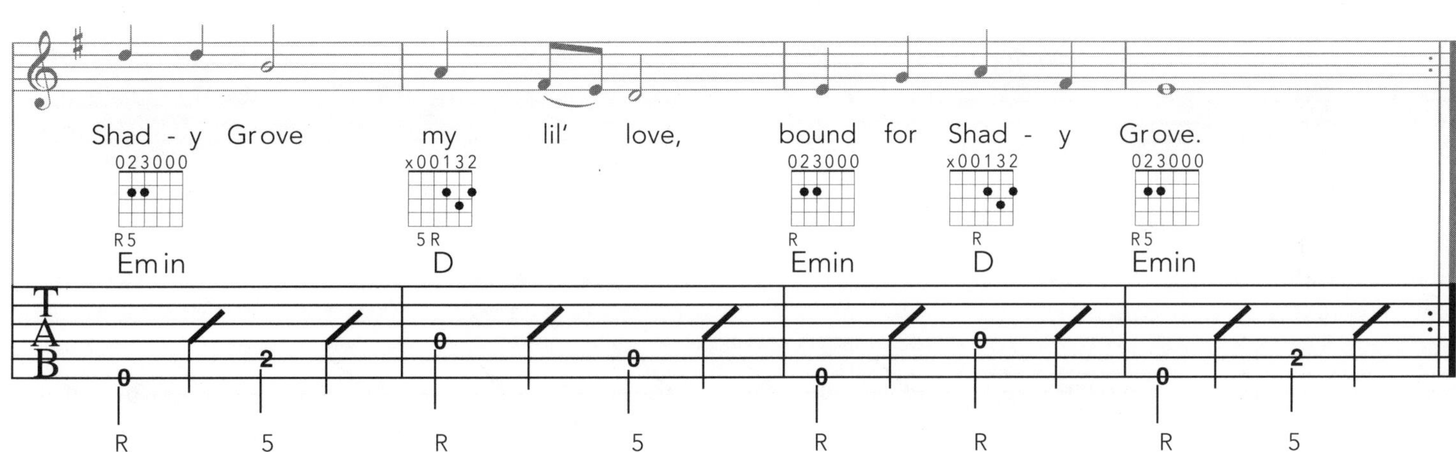

If we learn two more chords, a five-string C and D7, and put them together with the G chord that you already know, we will have the basic chord group for the key of G (G=I, C=IV, D=V). Check the diagrams below and learn the locations of the bass notes of each chord.

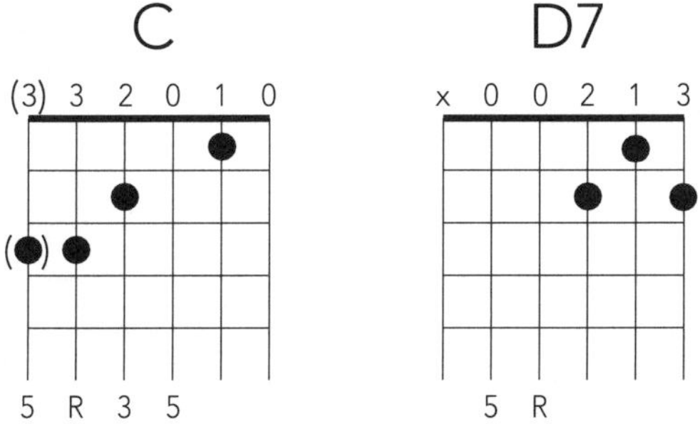

This exercise will help you get these chords under your fingers. When you want to use the 5th as a bass note on the C chord, you must move your 3rd finger to the 6th string.

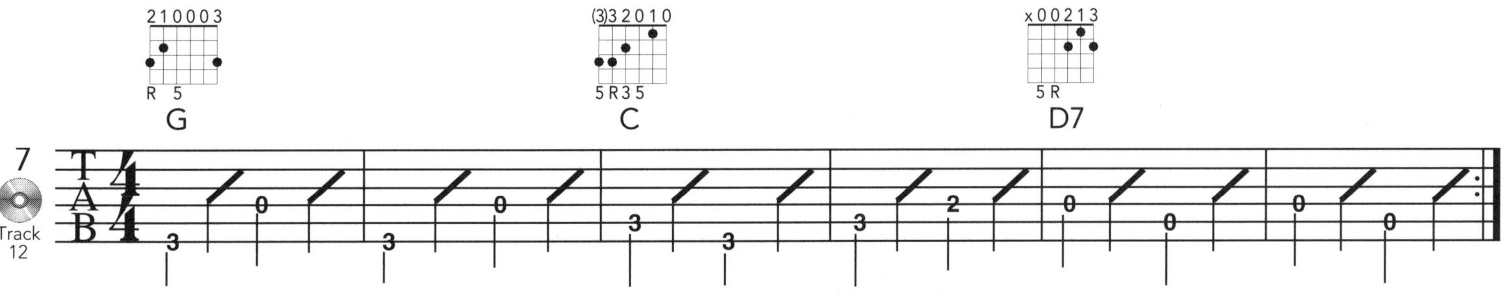

Your first song in the key of G is the classic, *John Henry*. Enjoy!

$\frac{3}{4}$ Time

Up until now, all the songs and examples in this book have been in $\frac{4}{4}$ time, four beats to the measure (see page 7 to review time signatures). We have created our guitar parts by alternating bass notes and chords to fill each measure: bass - chord - bass - chord. Many songs, however, are in $\frac{3}{4}$ time, and have three beats in each measure.

= Half-note strum

The easiest way to accompany in this time signature is to play bass - chord - chord in each measure. Strike the bass note on the first beat, and then strum the chord on beats two and three. If you alternate bass notes it will be between measures. Try the beautiful classic spiritual, *Amazing Grace*. Pay special attention to the 1st and 2nd endings at the bottom of the page.

Amazing Grace

Track 14

Traditional, Words by John Newton

* A dot next to a note means to increase it's value by one half. For instance, a half note equals two beats. Half of two is one, so a dotted half note equals three beats (𝅗𝅥 + ♩ = 𝅗𝅥.)

Chapter 4

Fingerstyle Chord Plucking and Bass Runs

PHOTO–COURTESY OF STAR FILE, INC.

Fingerstyle Chord Plucking

We can use the right hand fingers to pluck the strings instead of strumming with the back of the nails. The fingerstyle picture on the right will help you find a good playing position.

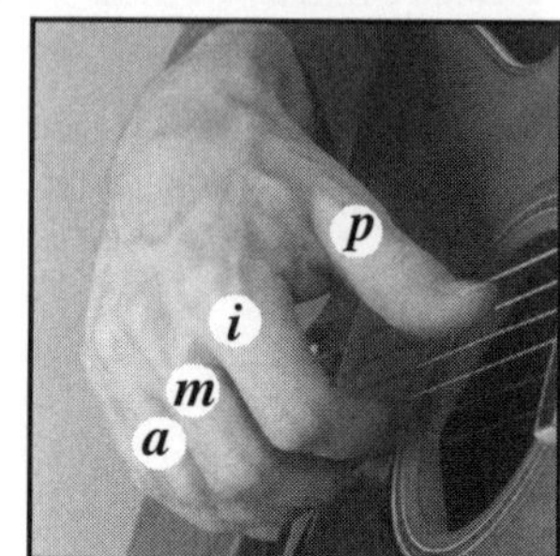

Since the 1960s, ***James Taylor,*** *has been one of the most popular performers in America. His distinctive approach to fingerstyle guitar is a large part of his unique sound.*

Use the index finger (*i*) to pluck the 3rd string, the middle finger (*m*) to pluck the 2nd string and the ring finger (*a*) to pluck the 1st string. Keep the fingers curled and use the left corner of the fingers to pluck the string with flesh and nail together. Keep the three fingers lightly touching each other and pluck towards the palm of your hand with the three fingers simultaneously. Keep your hand still—make it a finger motion not a hand motion. This technique gives a somewhat softer sound than strumming. Try Examples 8 and 9, and then try some of the songs you already know with this technique.

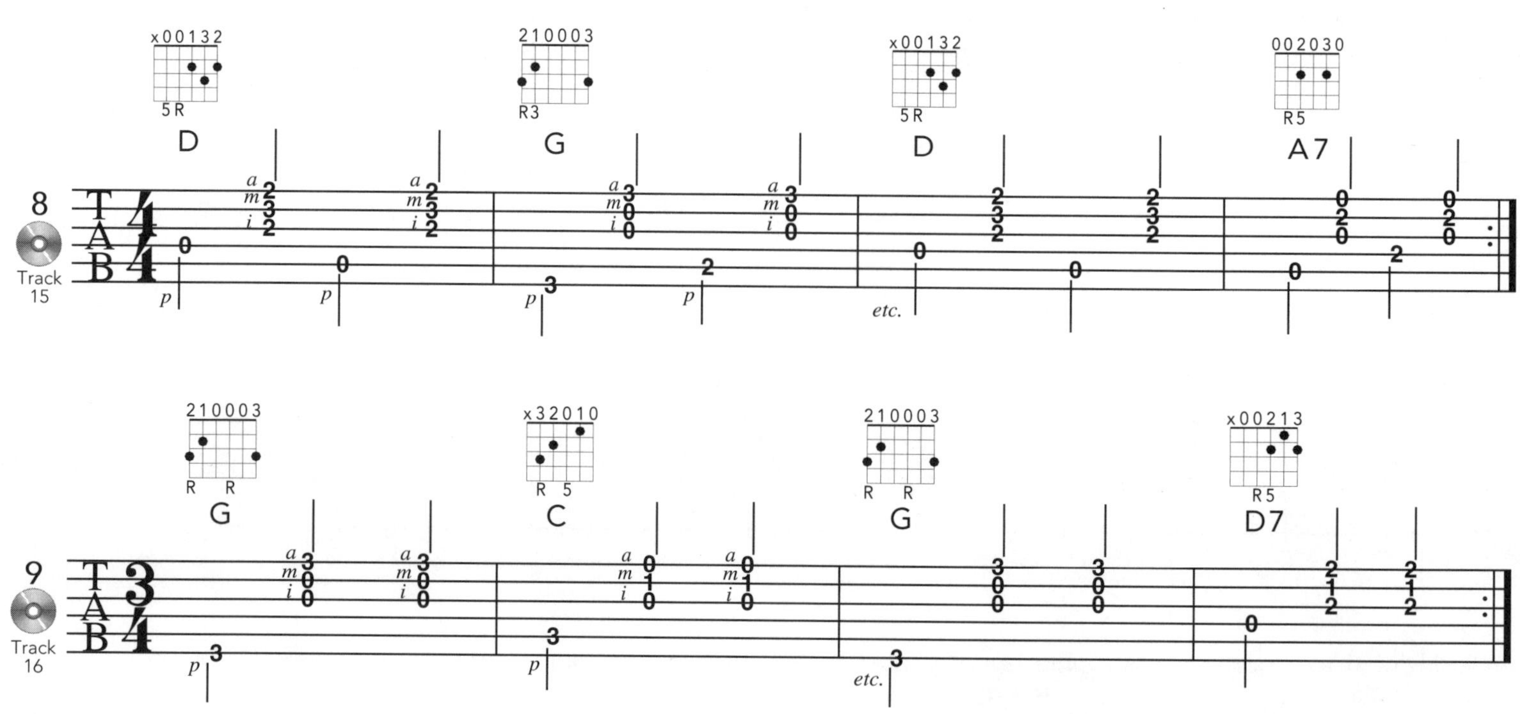

Bass Runs

Well, it's time to give your thumb (or your pick) a little more action. The old bass-chord-bass-chord accompaniment can get a little monotonous if over-used. To add variety to your playing, try using some *bass runs*. A bass run is a series of low notes that usually connect two chords. It happens right before the arrival of a new chord. Check out these examples of bass runs connecting the chords you have been using. You can use any technique you wish on the chords—pluck, strum with your nails or strum with a pick.

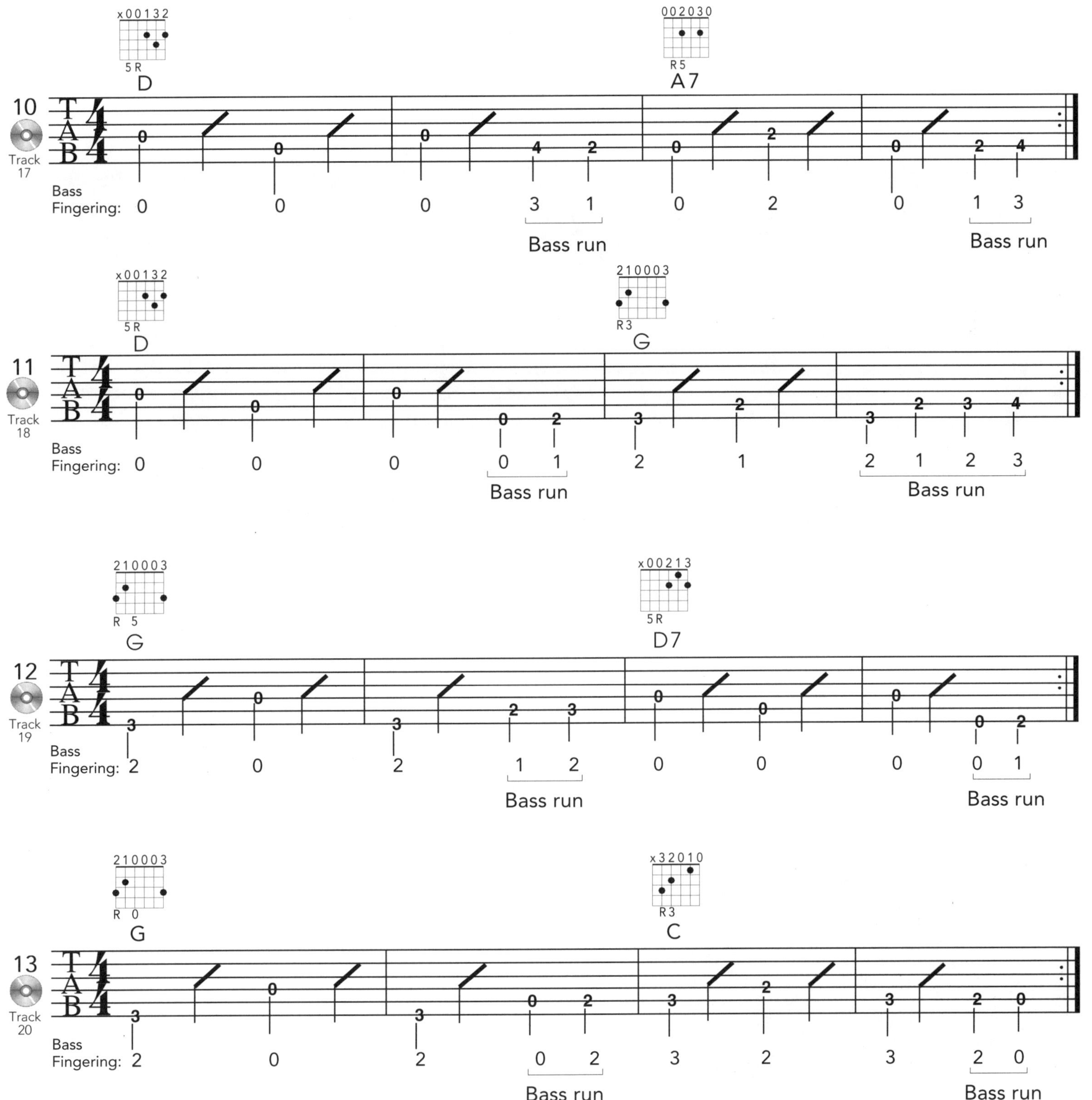

Once you have the idea, try adding some runs to the songs you have learned. It is not necessary to play every possible run all the time. Moderation and taste is the rule.

Chapter 5

Exploring Some New Keys

The Key of A

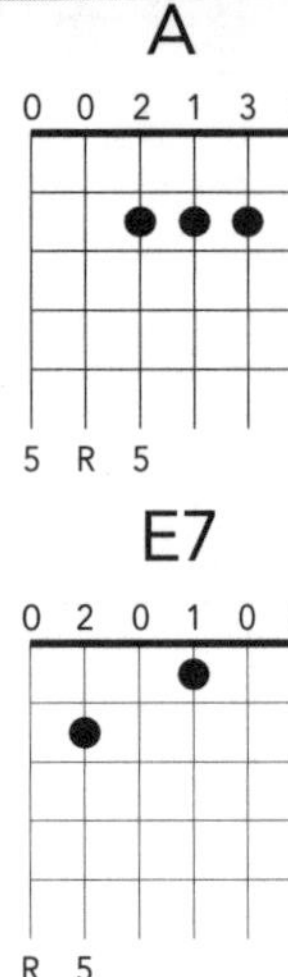

We have a few more chord groups to learn to complete our basic chord vocabulary. If we learn the A Major and E7 chords, and add in the D chord we already know, we will have the basic chord group for the Key of A.

The A Major chord can be fingered in a number of ways. I have found the best fingering for most applications is to play an A7 fingering and then squeeze your 1st finger in-between the 2nd and 3rd fingers. You should try to get the 1st finger as close to the fret as possible, but it won't be as close as the 2nd and 3rd fingers. The E7 chord is easy.

The alternating bass and bass run exercise below will introduce you to the key of A.

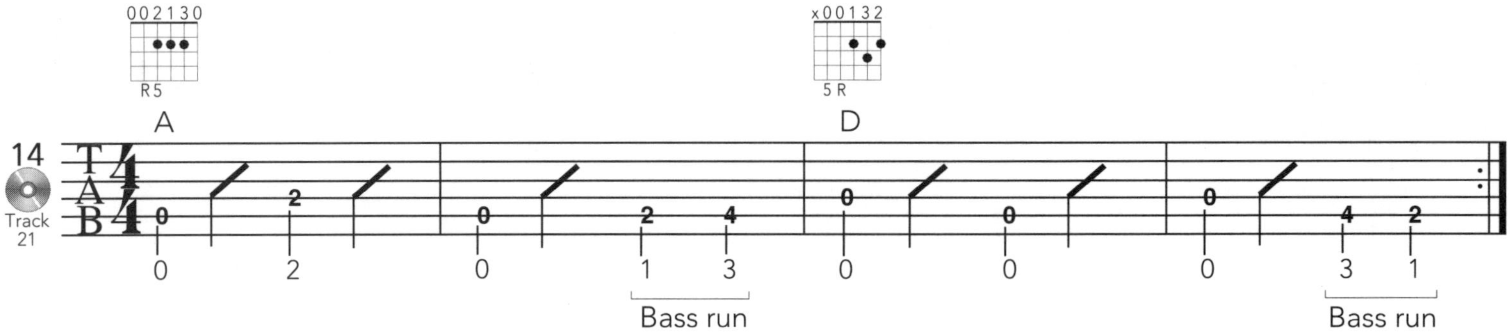

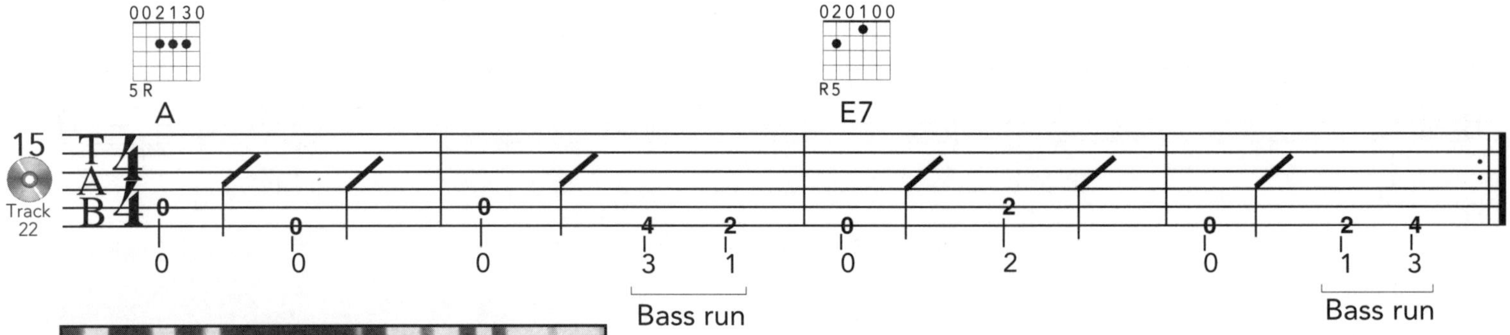

14 Track 21

A (002130, R5) — D (x00132, 5R)

0 2 | 0 1 3 (Bass run) | 0 0 | 0 3 1 (Bass run)

15 Track 22

A (002130, 5R) — E7 (020100, R5)

0 0 | 0 3 1 (Bass run) | 0 2 | 0 1 3 (Bass run)

PHOTO COURTESY OF THE COUNTRY MUSIC FOUNDATION

Country fingerpicker **Merle Travis** *is famous for his signature alternating bass pattern.*

Here is a full arrangement of *Careless Love* in A. Try it simply at first, without the bass runs, and then add the runs. If the melody is too low for your singing voice, try it with a capo on the 2nd or 3rd fret.

The Key of E

We have come to the "people's key," the key of E. This key really uses the meat of the guitar's range and open strings, from the lowest note on the instrument up through the 1st string and beyond. For that reason, thousands of songs for guitar, in every style of music, are written in this key. Try the E chord shown on the right.

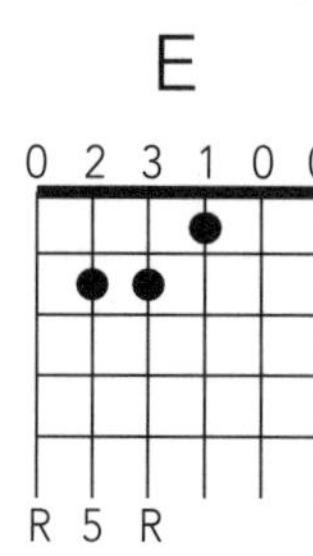

Here is an exercise that includes the alternating basses and bass runs in E changing to an A chord. Before trying the bass run, practice strumming through the chords.

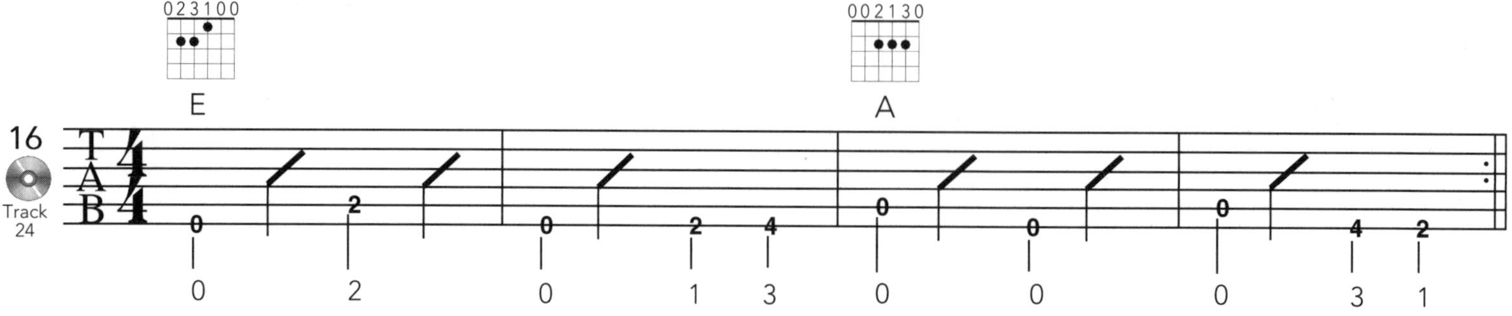

This next exercise introduces the B7 chord. Take your time forming this chord since is requires new stretches for the left-hand fingers.

Notice that when a 5th is desired in the bass of the B7, the 2nd finger can move to the 6th string, similar to what we did with the C chord on page 13. Play this next example very slowly to get used to the B7 chord.

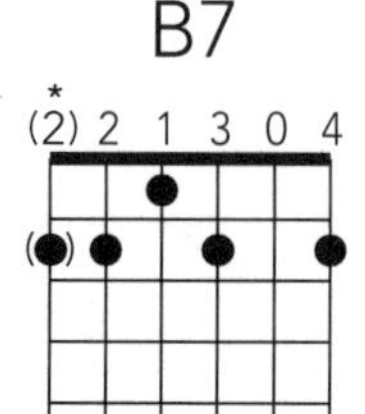

* The (2) is an alternate bass note.

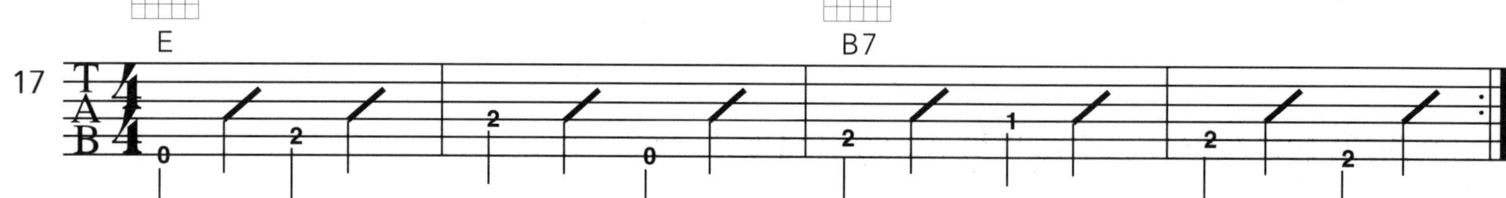

The Down/Up Strum

Let's also try something new with the right hand strum. We will use a bass-strum combination, but instead of just strumming down with the back of the nails, we will split the strum in half and come back up with a flick of the index finger. The resulting rhythm when coupled with the bass note is: boom - chick-a - boom - chick-a or 1 - 2 & - 3 - 4 &. The "and" is called the up-beat. Notes that divide beats into two parts are called *eighth notes* (see page 7). Make it a light, quick strum. You can use this rhythm as a change of pace from the single down strum. The can also be executed with a down/up pick strum.

⊓ = strum down with the back of the nail

V = strum up with a flick of the index finger.

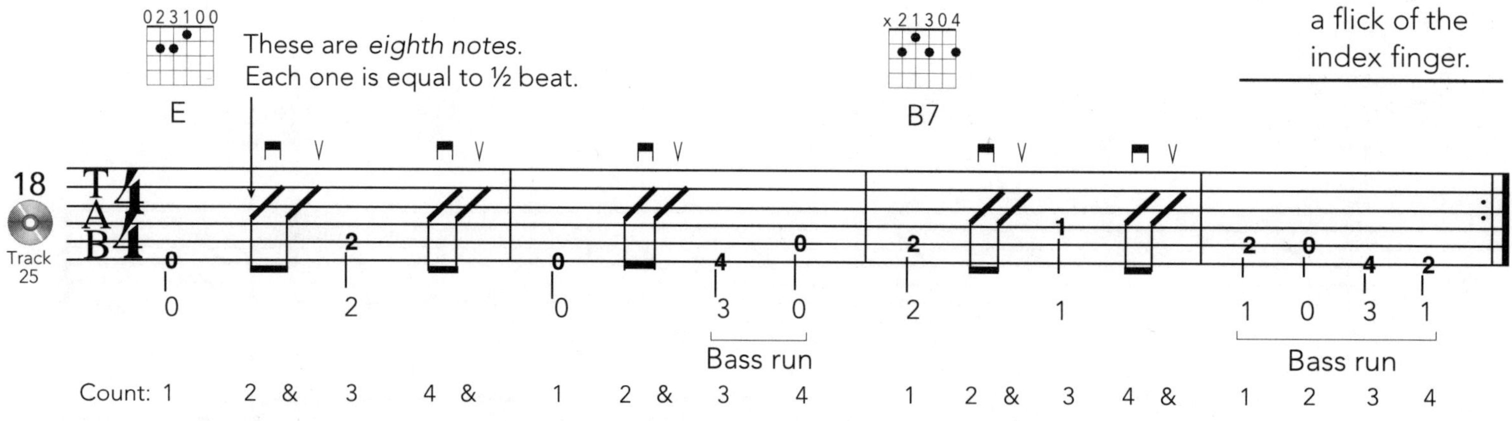

In *Will the Circle Be Unbroken*, the down/up strum is indicated all the way through. The down/up strum is done with *sixteenth notes*, which divide each beat into four parts (1-e-&-ah, see page 7). Here is an exercise to give you some practice with sixteenth notes. Set your metronome to a slow tempo and count aloud as you strum the E chord in the rhythm shown.

023100
E
19
1 2 & 3 e & ah 4 e & ah

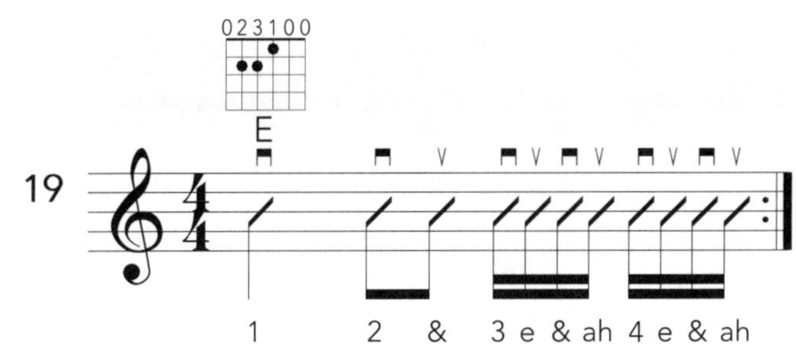

In the accompaniment rhythm of this song, play the 1st, 3rd and 4th parts of each beat, skipping the second pulse. Each beat should be counted "1 - & ah, 2 - & ah," etc.

Counting Eighths and Sixteenths

1 (e) & ah 2 (e) & ah

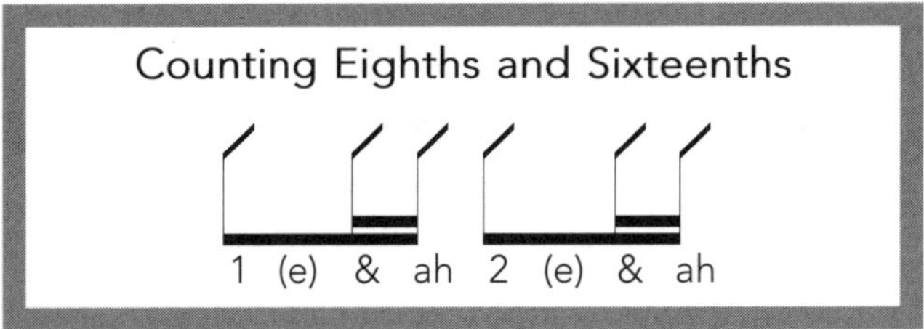

Will the Circle Be Unbroken

Track 26

Traditional

M.M. = 80

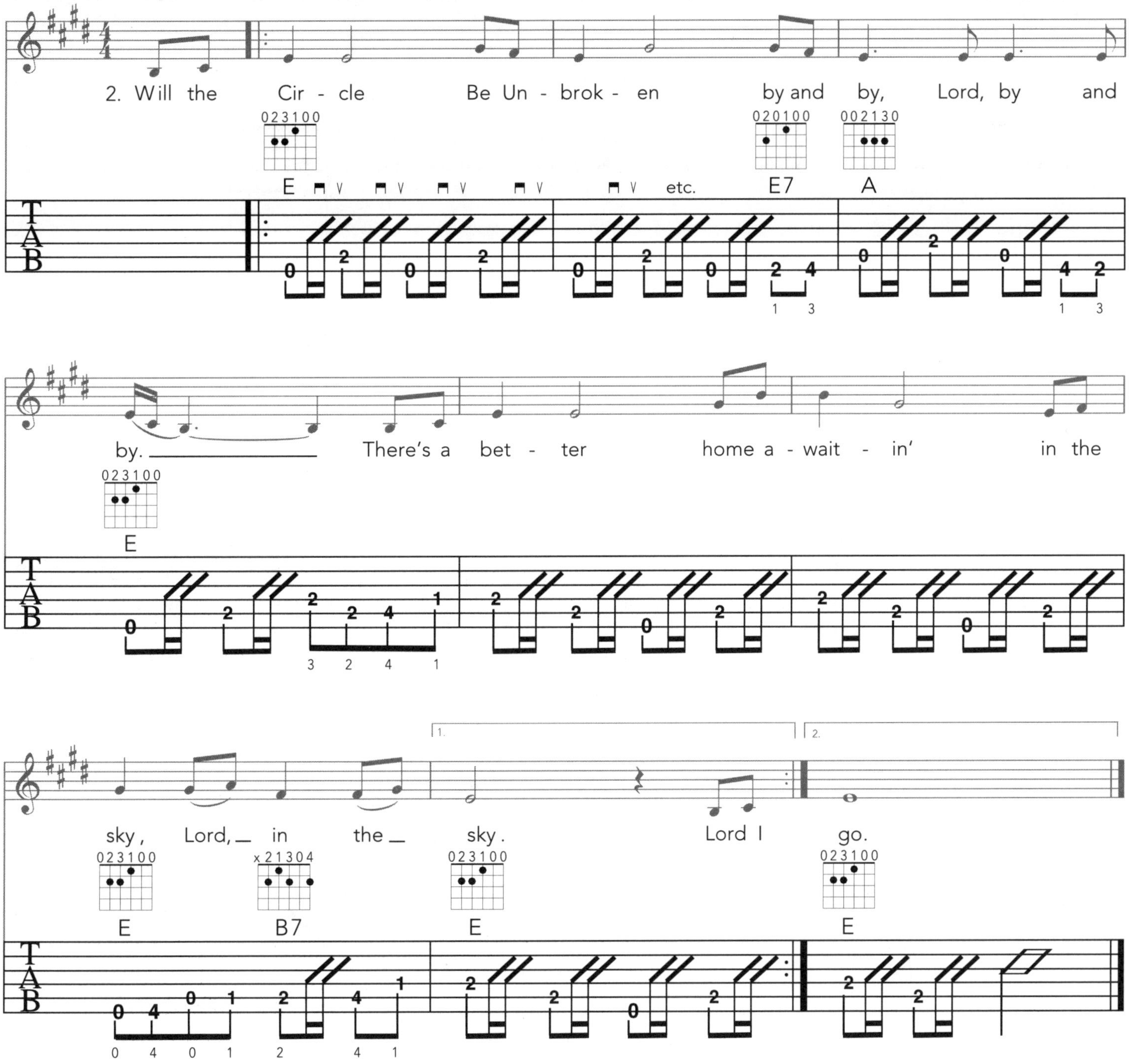

2. Will the Cir - cle Be Un - brok - en by and by, Lord, by and
E E7 A
etc.
by. There's a bet - ter home a - wait - in' in the
E
sky, Lord, in the sky. Lord I go.
E B7 E E
1. 2.

The Key of C

The key of C is usually the first key people learn to play on the piano because it uses all the white keys and is easy to read and play. On the guitar, however, the key of C is not the easiest key, so we have saved it for now, when your chord playing ability is more developed. The chord group for this key uses C along with two new chords, F and G7.

The F chord poses a new problem in that the left hand index finger must press down two strings at once. Before playing the F chord, practice fretting the 2nd and 1st strings at together:

When you feel confident about the index finger add the 2nd and 3rd fingers and try the full chord.

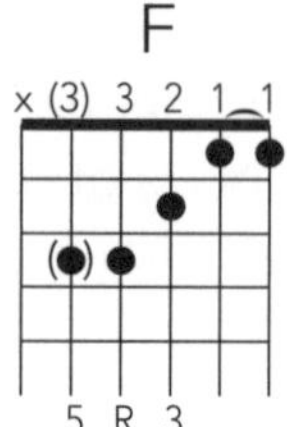

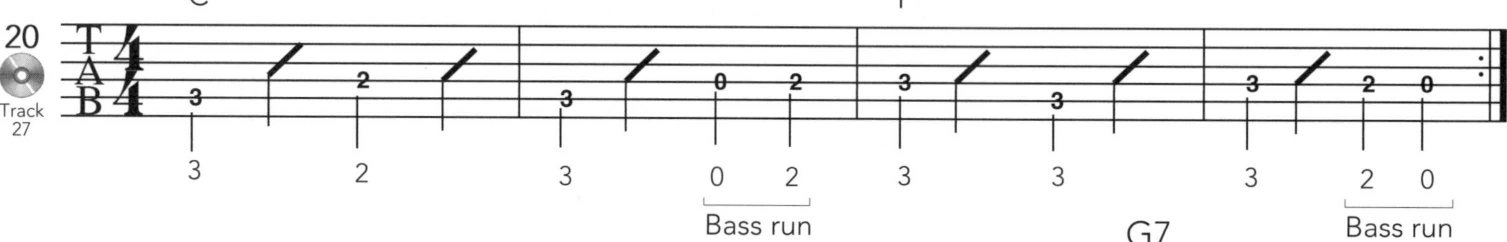

The G7 is similar to the basic C chord, but has a little wider stretch. Try this: Practice strumming through the chords in Example 21 before adding the bass runs.

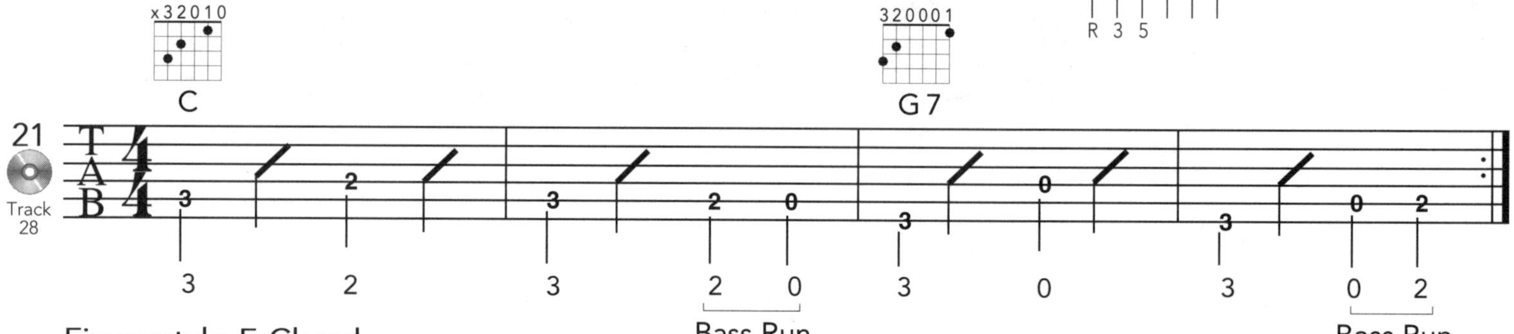

Fingerstyle F Chord

Many people use what is often called a "fingerstyle F chord," using the left-hand thumb to reach over the neck and fret the 1st fret on the 6th string. This may be a bit difficult to get the hang of at first, but it is well worth the effort. Most good fingerpickers, as well as country, rock and jazz players, often use the thumb to fret notes on the 6th string. Use the side of your thumb near the tip joint. Here is an exercise using this type of F chord.

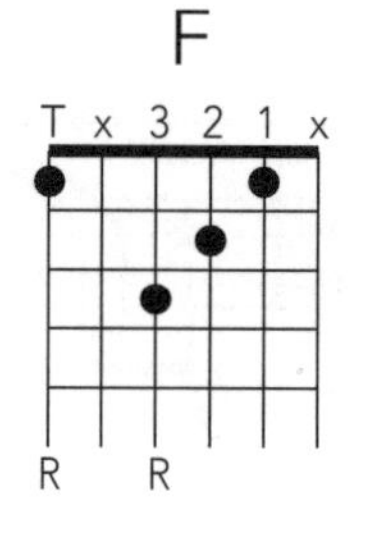

As an alternative to the fingerstyle F chord, try this barre chord. Put your left elbow in close to your body and lay your 1st finger across all six strings.

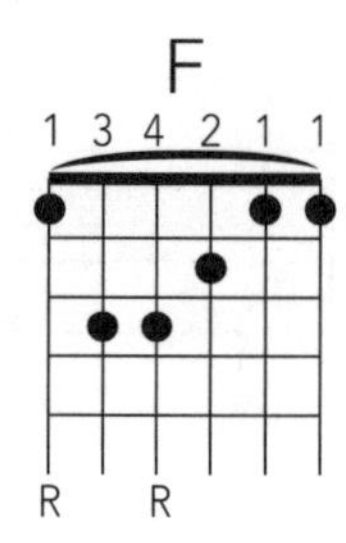

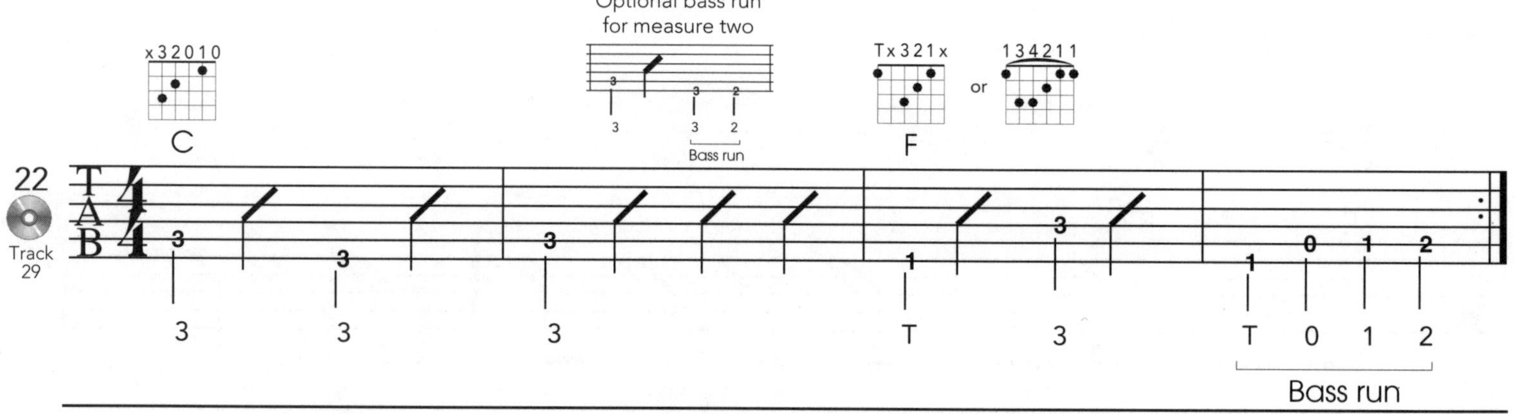

Now try *New River Train*, a song in C, using the fingerstyle F chord.

Chapter 6

New Chords and Right-Hand Techniques

You now know the primary chords in five keys. You've come a long way. Look for other songs that use these chords. Try all of the accompaniment techniques you've learned.

Transposing

Chord Group Chart

Key	I	IV	V
C	C	F	G7
G	G	C	D7
D	D	G	A7
A	A	D	E7
E	E	A	B7

Another way to change the pitch of a song, besides using the capo, is to actually change the key by using a different group of chords. This is called transposing. You can change the chords by looking at the Chord Group Chart and substituting the corresponding chords from another key. For example, if the song is in G, using G (I), C (IV) and D7 (V), you can change the chord group to the key of D by looking at the D row in the chart, and using the primary chords in that key— D (I), G (IV) and A7 (V)—instead.

New Minor Chords

So far, E minor is the only minor chord we have covered. Each of the keys shown in the Chord Group Chart can be expanded with minor chords. Let's learn three more common minor chords, A minor, D minor and B minor 7.

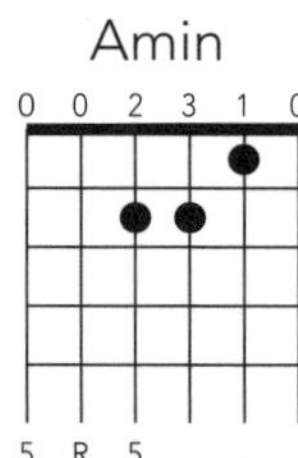

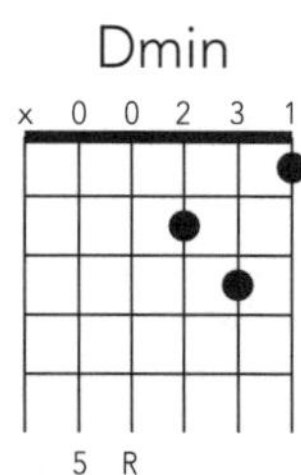

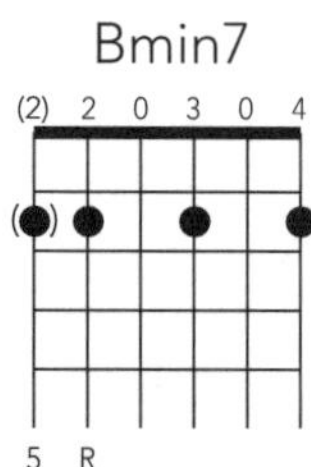

The Sixteenth Note Bass/Strum Pattern

While we are learning these new chords, let's expand on your right-hand technique. In Example 22, we will use sixteenth notes. A sixteenth note is equal to ¼ of a beat, so we can fit four notes into one beat. This means that we can fit a bass note and three strums into one beat. Example 23 uses some eighth notes too, and the resulting rhythm sounds like: boom–chick, boom-pa-chick-a, or 1–&, 2-e-&-ah, etc.

𝄎 = Repeat the previous measure

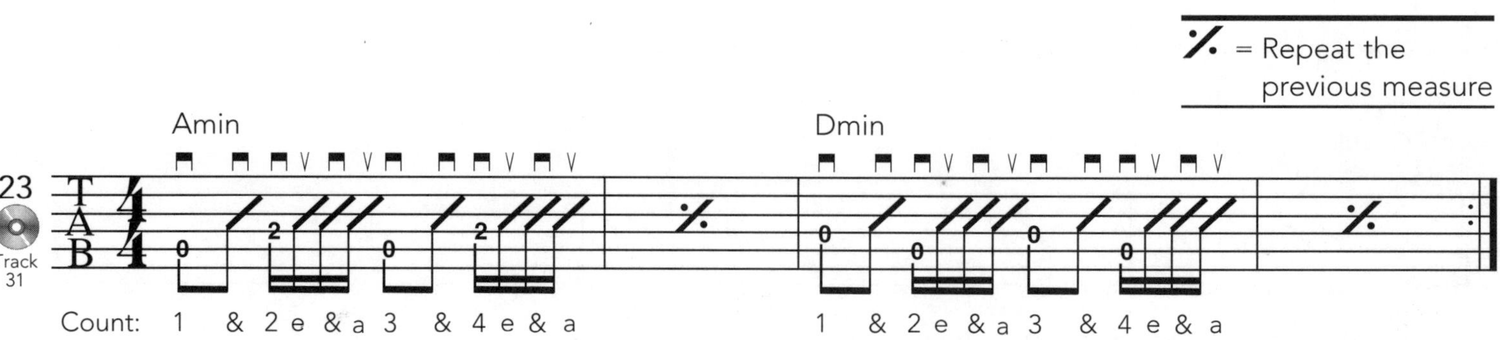

Wayfaring Stranger
M.M. = 76
Track 32
Traditional Spiritual
I'm just a poor Way-far-in' Strang-er a-travel-in' through this world of
Amin E Amin Dmin
woe, but there's no sick-ness no toil nor dan-ger in that bright
Amin E Amin E Amin
world to which I go. I'm go-ing there to see my
Dmin Emin Amin F G
fath-er. I'm go-ing there no more to roam. I'm just a-go-in' o-ver
C F Amin E Amin E
Jor-dan. I'm just a-go-in' ov-er home. I know dark home.
Amin G F Dmin Emin Amin Amin
T or 1 3 2
1. 2.

Arpeggio Picking

It's time to give those individual right-hand fingers a little more responsibility. We can use the right-hand thumb and fingers to strike the strings of a chord individually. This type of approach is called *arpeggio picking*. An arpeggio is a broken chord. The word comes from the Greek "*arpa*" meaning harp. Let's use a couple of the new minor chords along with C and G7 to play a basic arpeggio pattern.

Review of the right-hand fingers		
p	=	thumb
i	=	index
m	=	middle
a	=	ring.

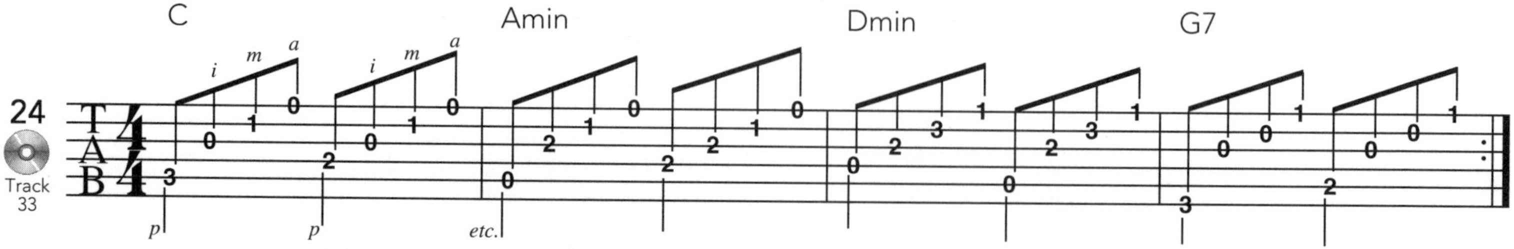

An arpeggio can be added to half of a measure with the other half remaining as a bass chord strum. Example 25 is the basis for the arramgement of *I Am A Pilgrim* on page 27. Notice that the rhythm is the same as the bass/strum pattern in *Wayfaring Stranger* on page 25.

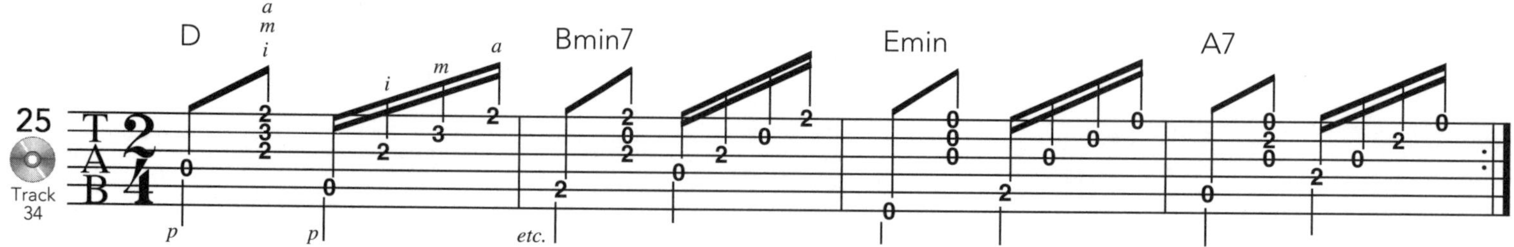

Many other arpeggio patterns are possible. Over the course of the next few songs you will see how some of these patterns can be used. Example 26A is a great pattern for slow to medium tempos. Example 26B is similar to the pattern used in *Greensleeves* on page 28.

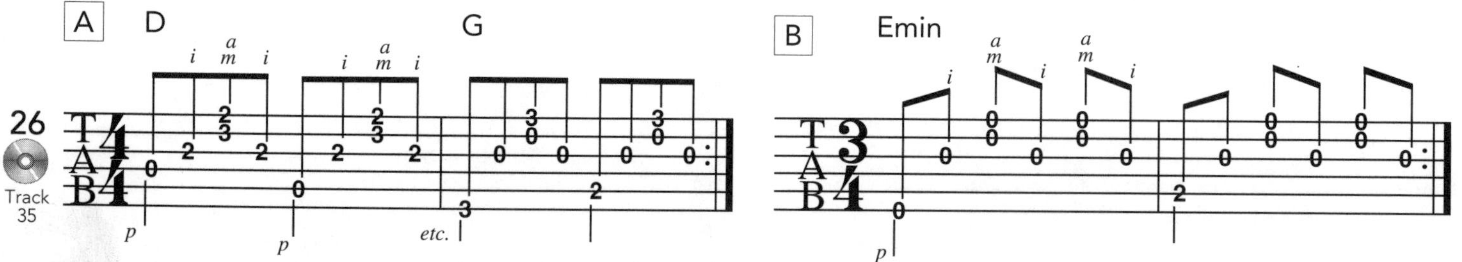

Another time signature in common use, especially in tunes derived from the Irish and other British Isles traditions, is $\frac{6}{8}$ time. In this type of rhythm, two main pulses are divided into three beats each: **1** 2 3, **4** 5 6. Tap your foot on 1 and 4. A three-finger pattern of *p - i - m* is an obvious choice for playing this rhythm, as in Example 27A. Example 27B shows a possible pick-strum. The second half of each measure uses a rhythm that strikes the first and third notes of each pulse. The arrows represent foot-taps.

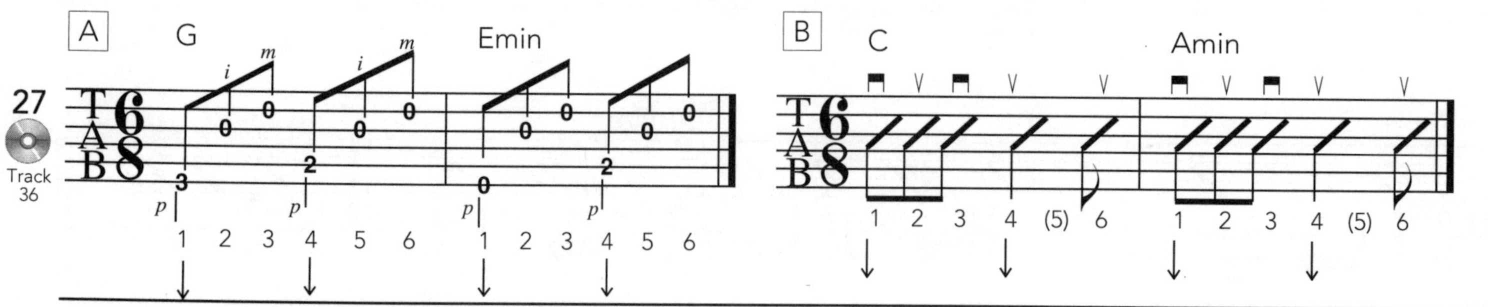

I Am a Pilgrim

Track 37

Traditional

For this song, learn to play both parts. Play along with the CD or find a friend to play with. Enjoy!

Greensleeves (instrumental)

Track 38

English Traditional

M.M. = 46 (two pulses per measure)

8va

1st Guitar

2nd Guitar

Emin D G D Bmin7 Emin Amin B7

i m a i m a i i m a i m a i i m a i m a i

p p p p etc.

(8va)

Emin D G D Bmin7 Emin B7 Emin

(8va)

G D Bmin7 Emin Amin B7

(8va)

1. 2.

G D Bmin7 Emin B7 Emin Emin

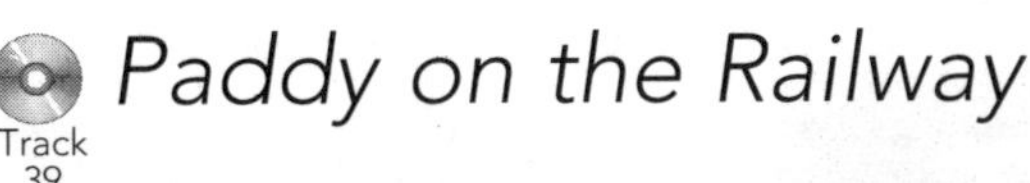

Paddy on the Railway

Traditional

M.M. = **108** (two pulses per measure)

1. In eigh - teen hun - dred and for - ty - one I put my cord - u - roy brich - es on.

Amin C

p p p p etc.

Put my cor - du - roy britch - es on to work up - on the rail - way.

Amin G Amin

Fi - li - mi - oo - ri - oo - ri aye. Fi - li - mi - oo - ri - oo - ri - aye.

Amin C

Fi - li - mi - oo - ri - oo - ri - aye. To work up - on the rail - way. In rail - way.

Amin G Amin Amin

1. 2.

Left-Hand Techniques and Syncopation

So, how is that right hand doing with arpeggios and strumming? If you have any trouble with the songs you are trying to play, simplify the accompaniment and use one of the easier techniques. When you have the song down, then add the complete right hand.

Meanwhile, there are a couple of other things that we need to discuss in regard to your left hand: hammer-ons, pull-offs and slides. All of these techniques are written with slurs ⌒. They create a smooth, flowing effect. Make sure you keep good time, and use your imagination when applying techniques such as these to your songs.

Hammer-Ons

A hammer-on is produced by striking an open or fretted note and then hammering down on a new note on the same string with another finger of your left hand. The result is sounding a higher note without striking the string again with your right hand. This is easiest when the note preceding the hammer-on is an open note. Try the following exercise using some of our basic chord positions to get the idea. *Don't This Road Look Rough and Rocky*, on the next page, uses this technique coupled with an arpeggio to create a nice pattern.

H = Hammer-on

28

Track 40

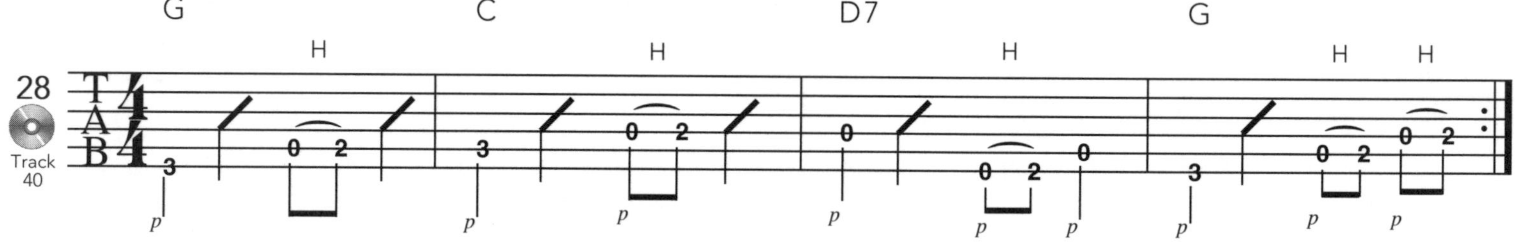

Pull-Offs and Slides

A pull-off is the opposite of a hammer-on. A fretted note is struck and then the left hand finger flicks downward (towards the floor) off the string, sounding a lower note without the right hand striking the string again. In a slide, the left hand slides either up or down to a new note, with or without the right hand restriking the string. The following example uses these two techniques.

P= Pull-off
S = Slide
⁄= Slide up

29

Track 41

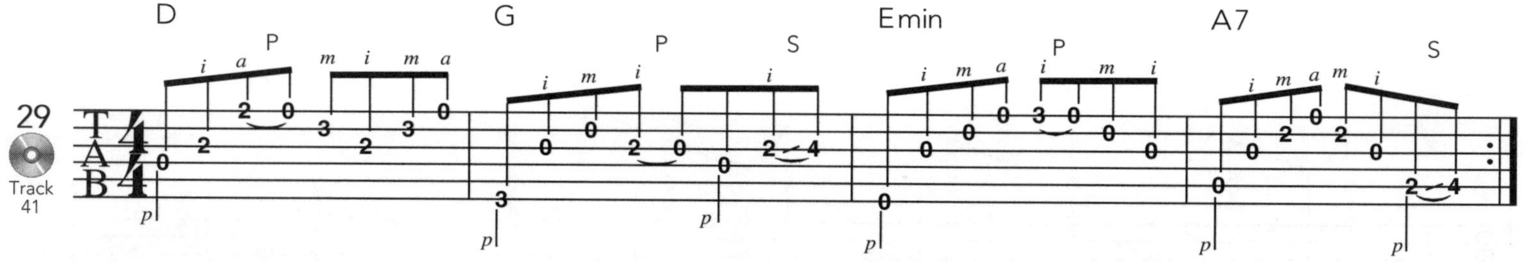

Don't This Road Look Rough and Rocky

Track 42

M.M. = 84

Traditional Spiritual

Another way to create syncopation is to use ties to break up a steady series of eighth notes. When notes are tied, the second note value is added to the first and not struck. Be sure to keep the down and up strokes in the right place. In TAB, ties are indicated with parentheses. A note or chord in parenthesis is tied to the

Syncopation

Syncopation is an important component of rhythm in nearly all styles of music. One style in particular is Calypso (*Sloop John B.* on page 33 is a good example of Calypso style). Syncopation means to shift an accent to weak beat or weak part of a beat where one is not expected. If you repeatedly play a straight quarter note strum, and leave out the third strum of each group of four, you will have a syncopation. If you count "1 & 2 &, etc., the "1" and the "2" are strong parts of the beat. The "&s" are the weak parts. Playing on the "&s" instead of the "1" and the "2" would be a syncopation. We think of this as "off the beat."

Try these basic syncopations. Use a pick for example 30. Notice that you will be strumming steady eighth notes, but leaving out the note on the 3rd beat.

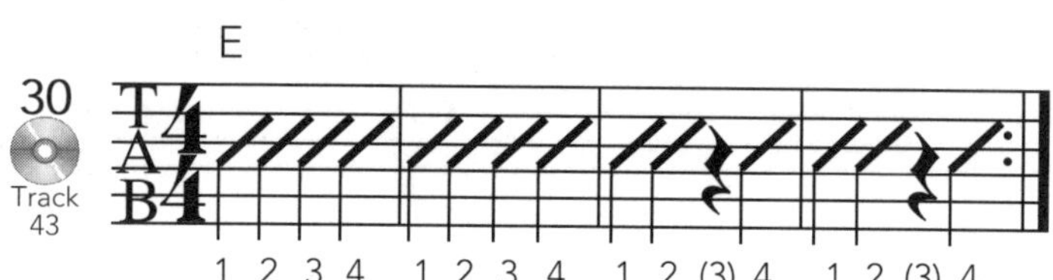

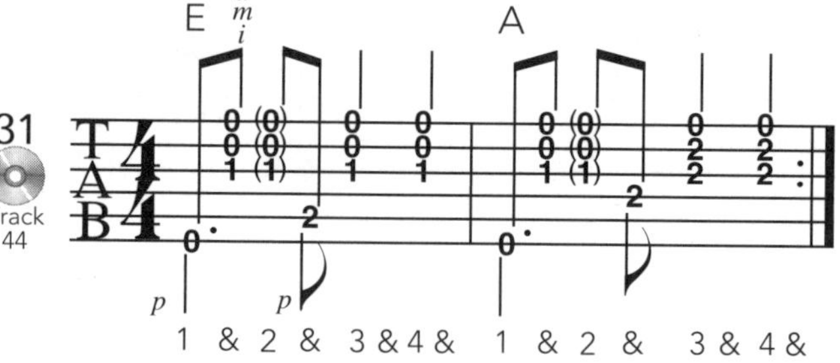

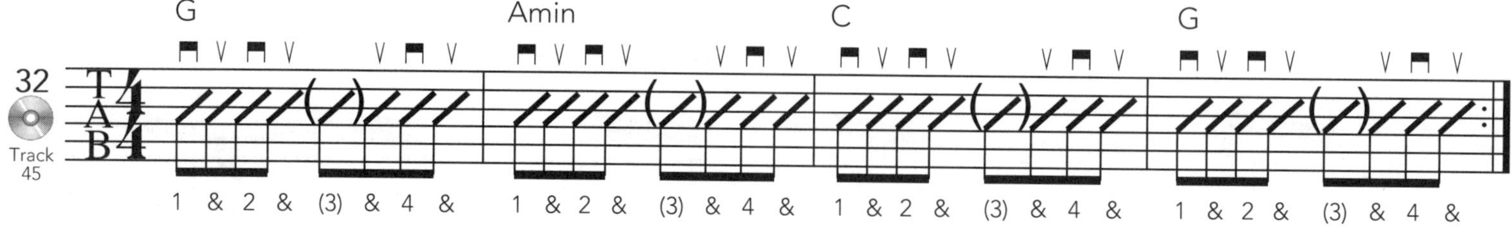

Example 33 uses a tie to syncopate an arpeggio pattern. In Example 32 group the eighth notes into an uneven grouping of 123-123-12.

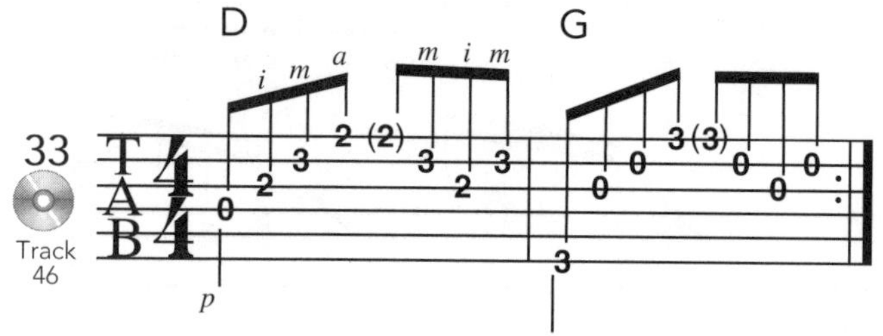

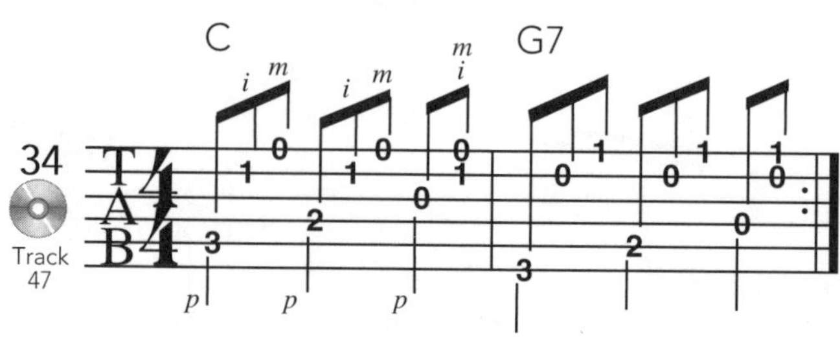

In Example 35 we are plucking very short notes on "&" counts and skipping most of the down beats (numbered beats). This is common in Reggae music. To create the short, plucked chords, release left hand pressure right after the pluck, but stay in contact with the strings.

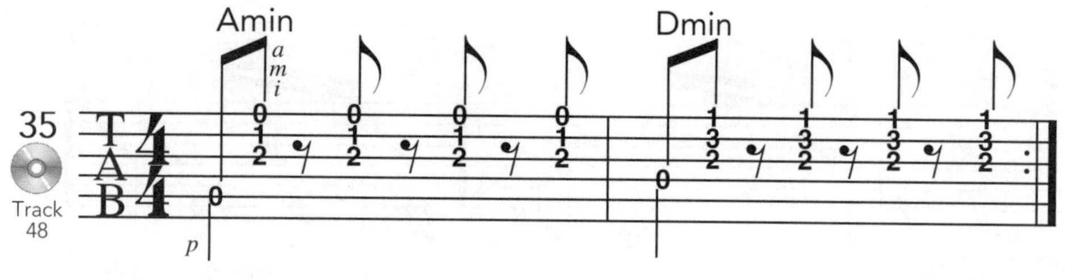

𝄾 = Eighth rest. This symbol indicates a half beat of silence.

Sloop John B.

Track 49

Traditional Bahaman

Chapter 8

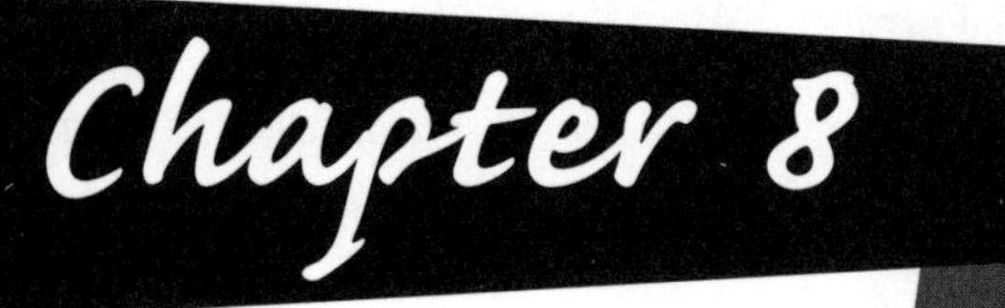

The Carter Family Style

The Carter Family is a vocal and instrumental group from Virginia that had an illustrious recording career during the 1930s and '40s. Mother Maybelle Carter developed a guitar style that has influenced countless folk and country guitar players over the years. Starting with an accompanimental rhythm of bass down-chord, up-chord, bass down-chord, up-chord, she would play melodies on the lower strings of the guitar and fill in the rhythm whenever a long note in the melody would allow. In this way, she played melody and accompaniment together. She probably used a thumb pick and her fingers to accomplish this, but it works great with a flat pick too. The following arrangement of *Wildwood Flower* is a great example of this type of playing. Bring out the melody and don't hit the chords too hard. The melody notes are circled in gray.

⊓ = Strum down
V = Strum up
(2) = Melody note

Wildwood Flower

Track 50

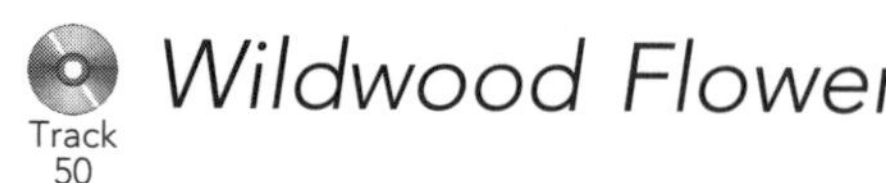

M.M. = *168*

Traditional, M. Irving & J.B. Webster

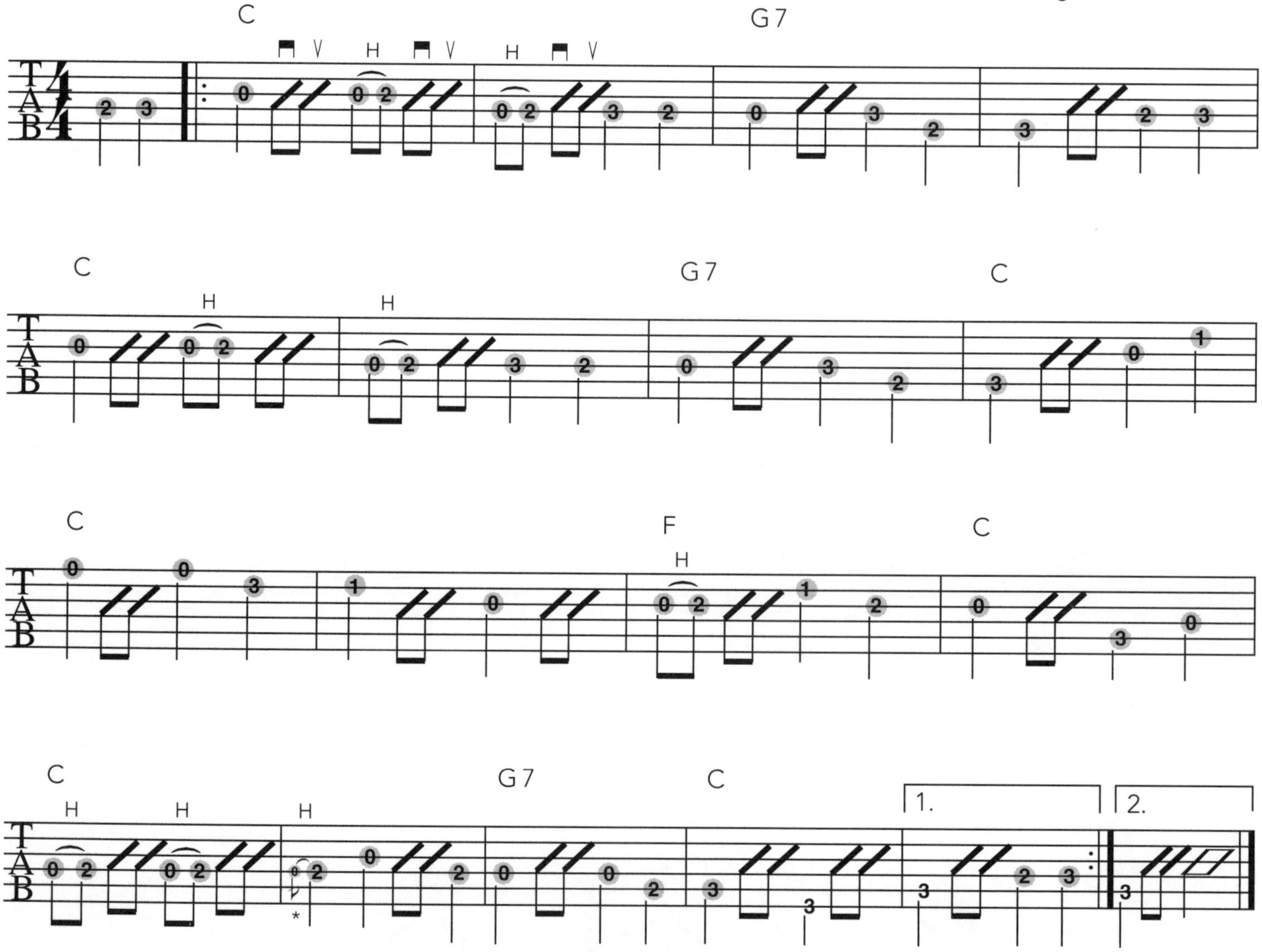

C
G7
C
G7
C
C
F
C
C
G7
C
1.
2.

* This is a grace note. A grace note is a quick, decorative note. In this style of music, grace notes are played directly on the beat.

Here is an arrangement of *Creole Belle* in G in the style of the Carter Family. Use a flat pick or your thumb to hit the bass melody and strum the down-ups with your pick or fingers. Again, the melody notes are circled in gray.

Traditional

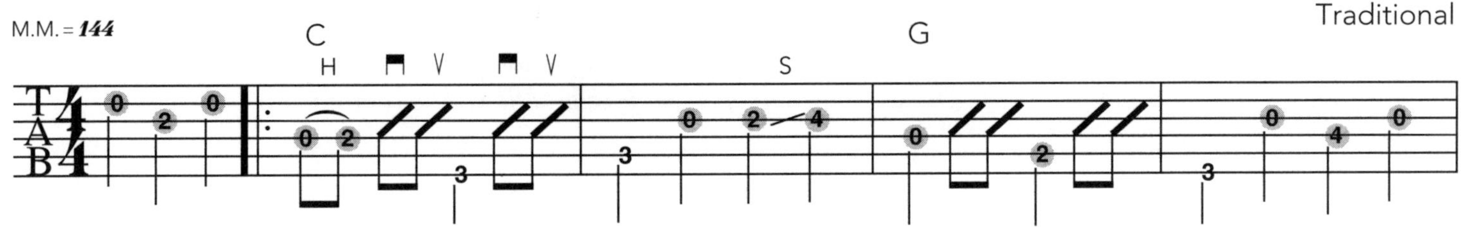

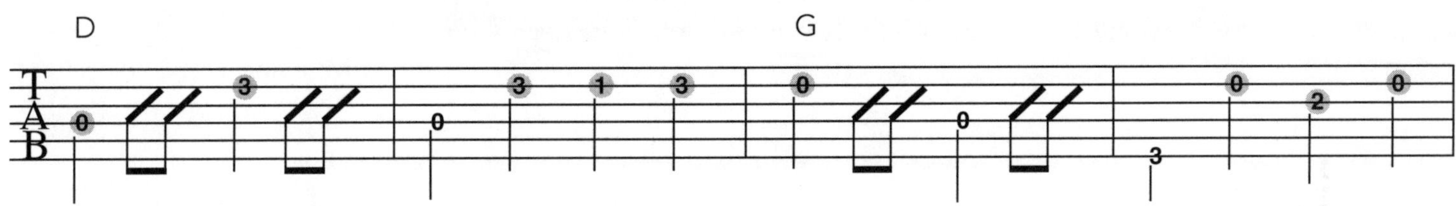

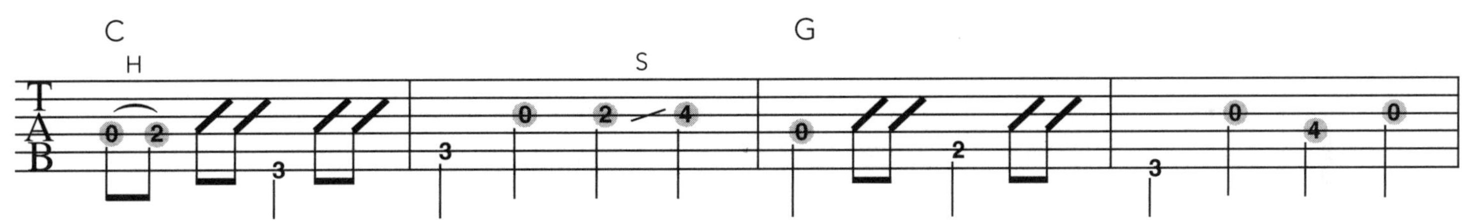

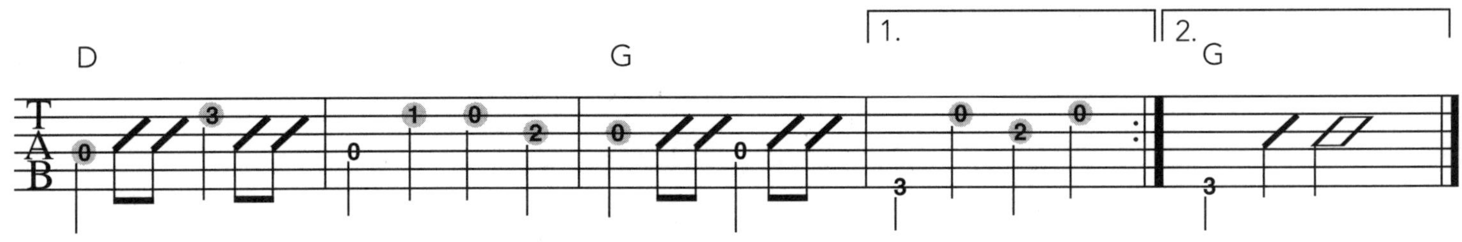

Blues and the Shuffle Rhythm

One of the most important influences on just about every style of American music is the blues. The blues is a musical tradition springing from the fusion of African and early American musical styles. The African singing style brought blue notes, notes that are just outside the key. These notes add tension and interest to the songs, and you will hear some of them in the upcoming songs. The blues also has a *swing* or *shuffle* to the rhythm that you will find in many folk songs.

The Shuffle–Let's Swing!

The *shuffle* or *swing eighths* rhythm is based on an underlying feel of triplets on each beat. A triplet is a division of the beat into three equal eighth notes, similar to what we did in $\frac{6}{8}$ time.

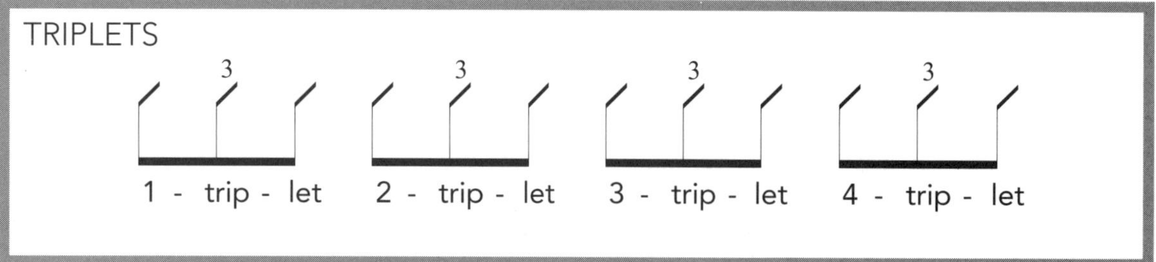

The shuffle is realized by articulating the first and third notes of each triplet creating:

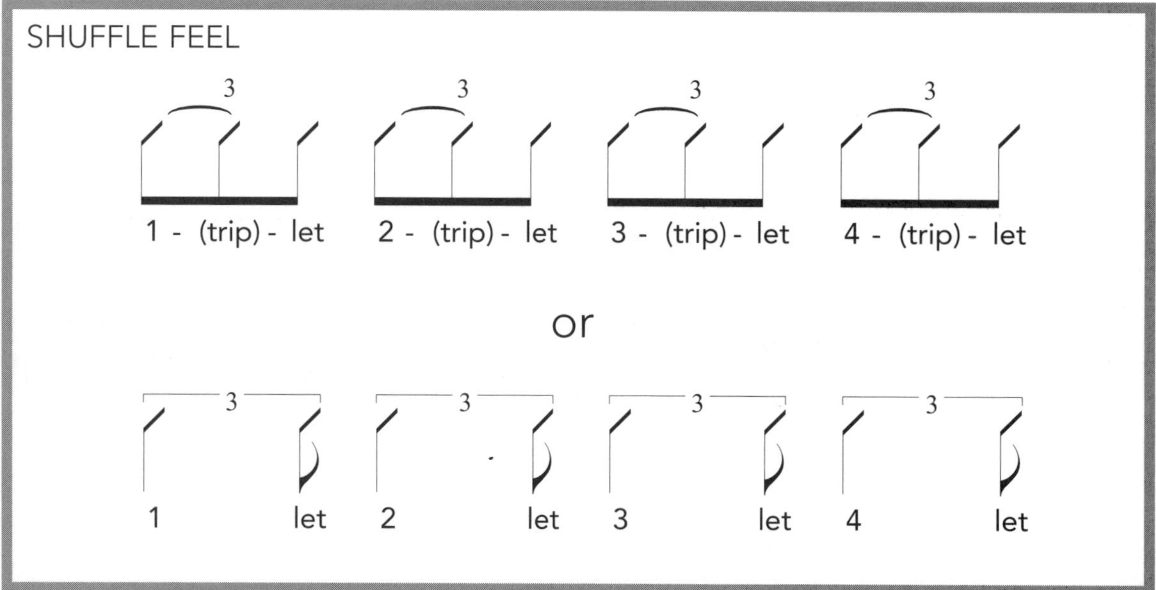

Notice that the first note of each pair is longer than the second, not evenly spaced like regular, *straight eighth notes.* As you will see in *Blues in A* on page 37, shuffles are usually written to look like regular, straight eighths. Blues and jazz musicians would automatically *swing the eighths.* In this book, we will mark the music "Shuffle" when its time to swing.

The blues has also brought us certain song *forms* (the form of a song is its organization or order of events) that are very commonly used in all styles. The *twelve bar blues* and the *eight bar blues* are two of these forms.

The following example is the accompaniment to a twelve bar blues form in the key of A. You will notice that it is twelve measures long; hence the name of the form. It uses two-note chords that are standard in this style. Use your 1st finger to hold down the 2nd fret notes and use your 3rd finger for the 4th fret notes. The other note in each chord is open. Remember the shuffle feel and use all down strokes of your pick or thumb.

Blues in A

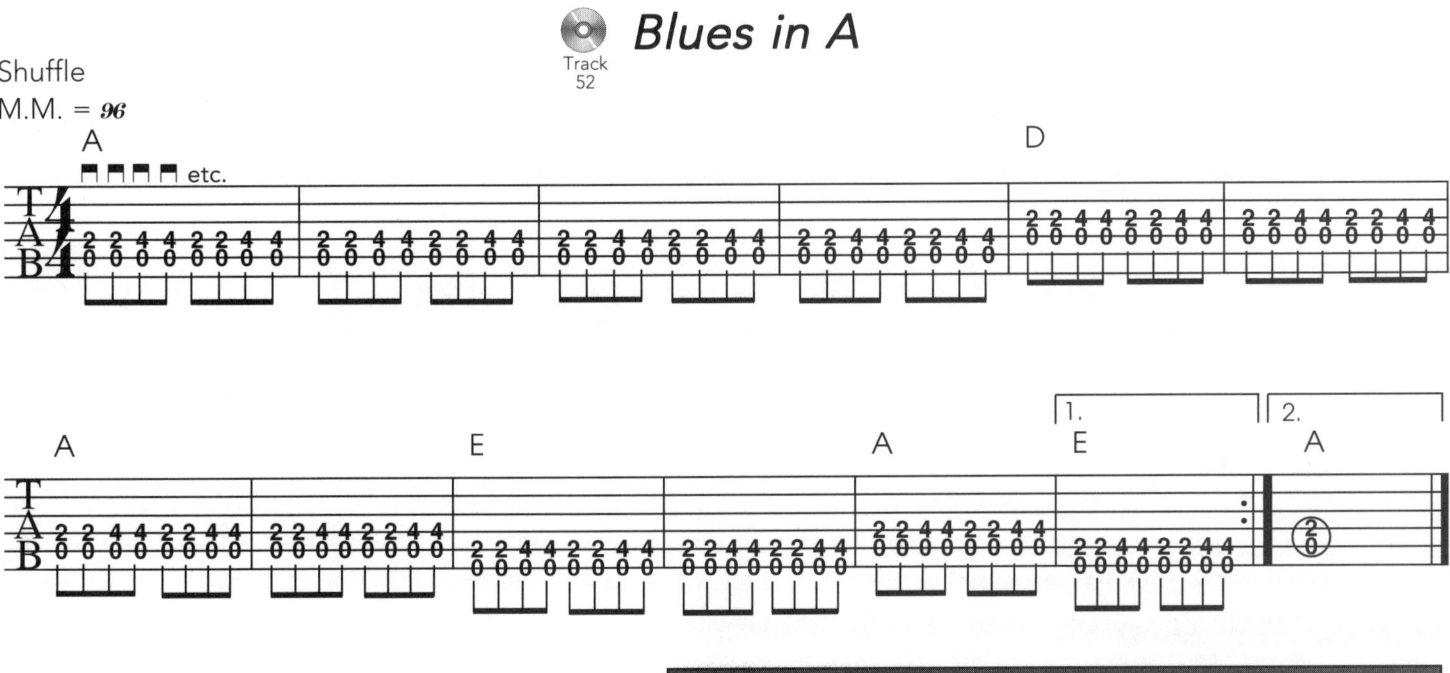

PHOTO–MARK HARLAN\COURTESY OF STAR FILES, INC.

Since the 1960s, ***Bob Dylan*** *has written and recorded a vast catalog of great songs. His lyrical genius has influenced several generations of songwriters, and made him an indelible figure in American popular music.*

Frankie and Johnny

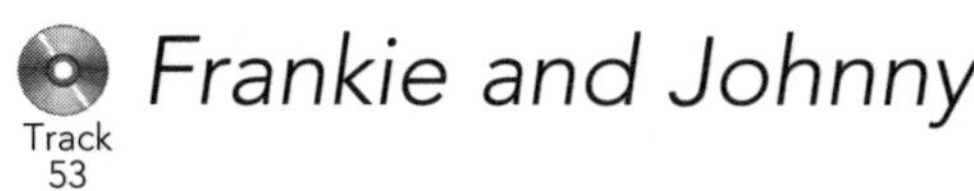

M.M. = *104*

Traditional

Shuffle

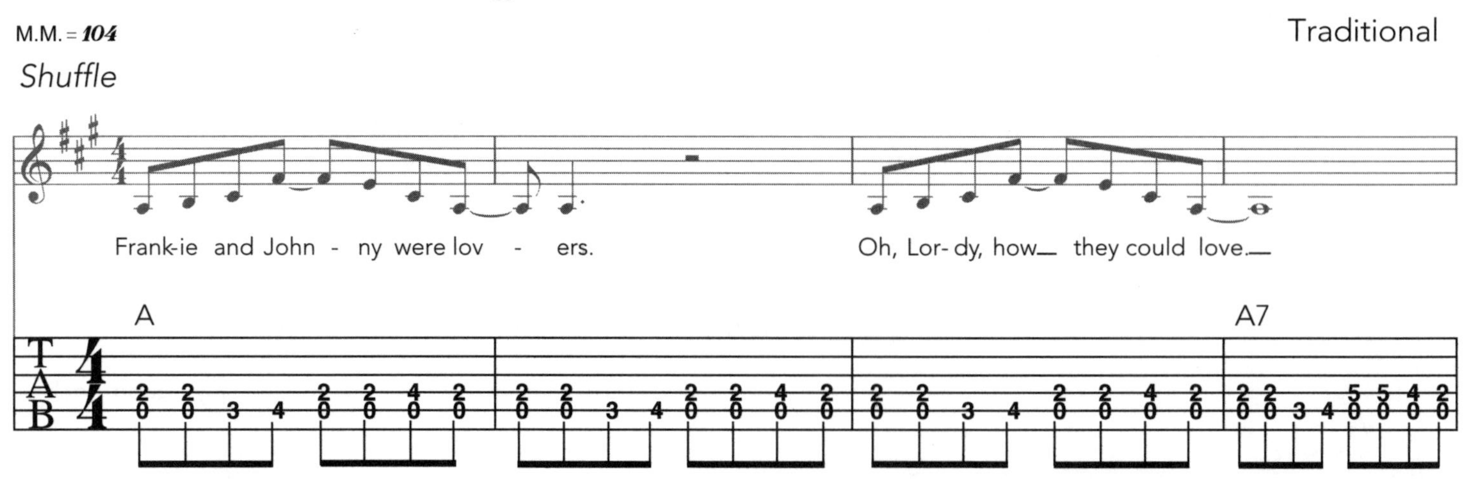

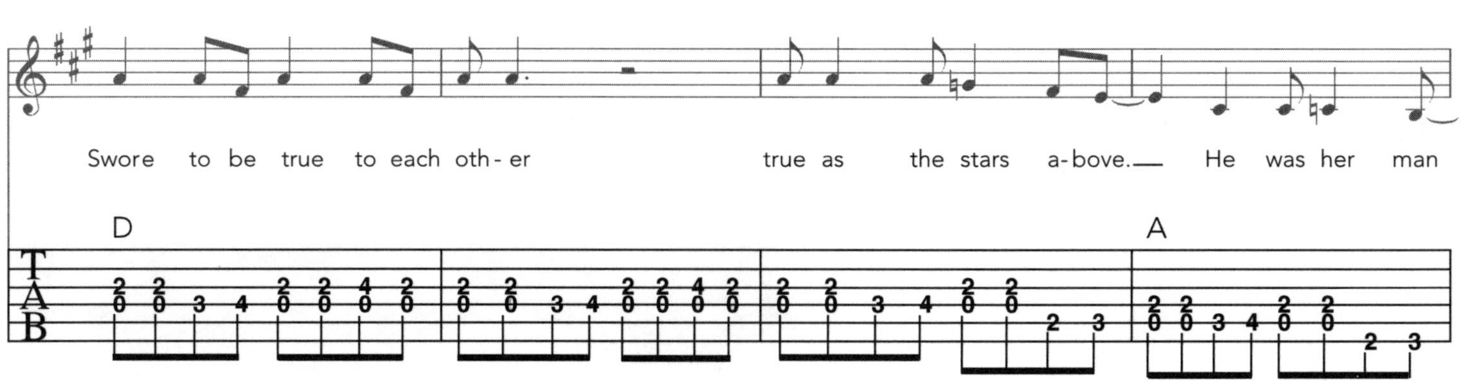

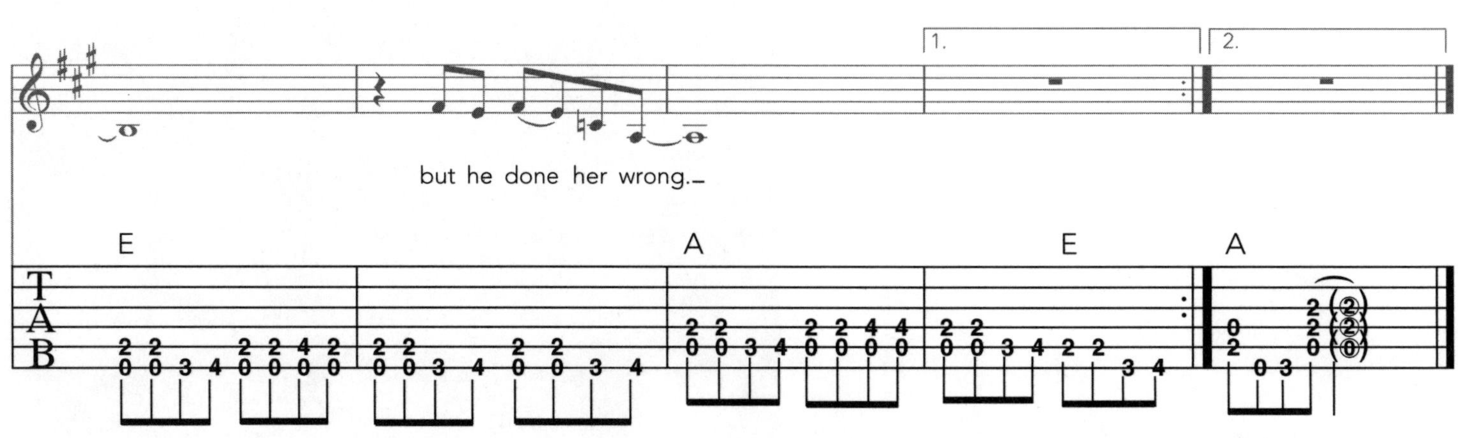

The shuffle feel can be applied to our basic bass-down-up or bass-up-down-up strum. Try this on the blues standard *Sittin' on Top of the World*. We will also use a variation of the G chord called G5 which is very common in many styles of bluegrass and rock.

G5
2 x 0 0 3 4
R

x = Mute 5th string with 2nd finger.

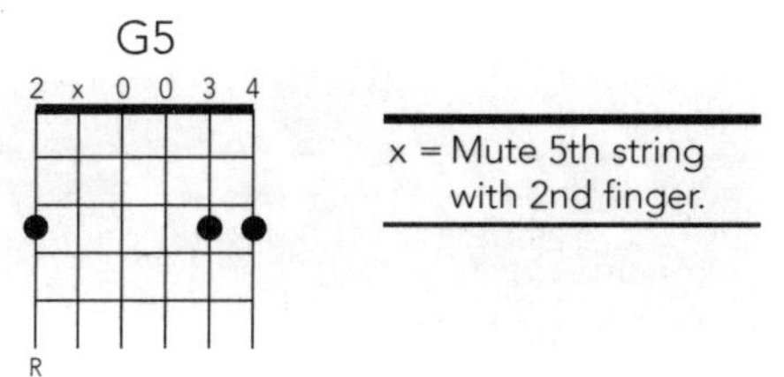

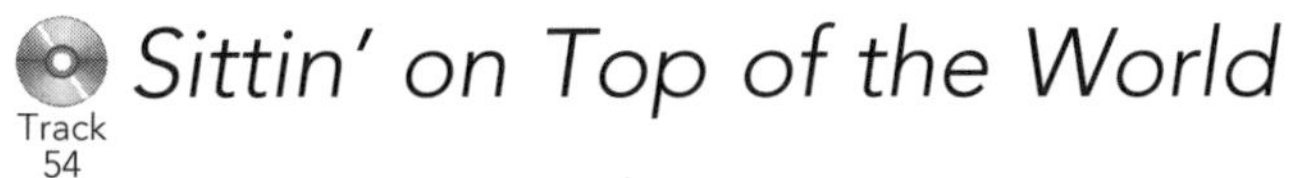

Sittin' on Top of the World

Track 54

M.M. = 144

Shuffle

Traditional

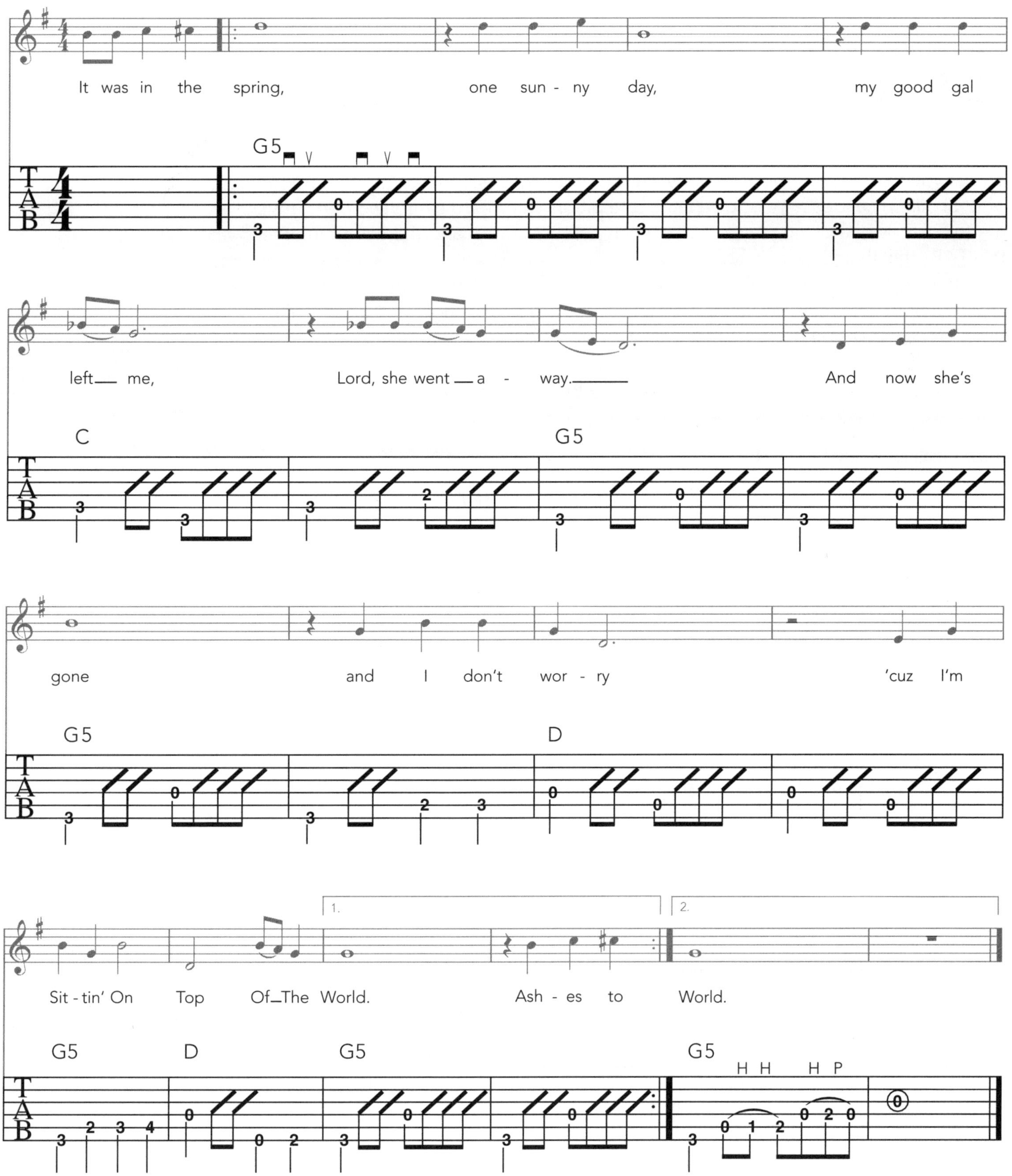

It was in the spring, one sun - ny day, my good gal
G5
left — me, Lord, she went — a - way. — And now she's
C G5
gone and I don't wor - ry 'cuz I'm
G5 D
Sit - tin' On Top Of — The World. Ash - es to World.
G5 D G5 G5
1. 2.
H H H P

Chapter 10

Melody Picking

If you have been playing most of the examples in this book with a flat pick, it's time to put it down and get those right-hand fingers in gear. Make sure you have tried the arpeggio picking in Chapter 6 before you continue.

Our next approach is called melody style fingerpicking, Travis picking (after Merle Travis, the great country guitar player who popularized this style) or country-blues picking. Some of the other great practitioners of this style are Elizabeth Cotton, Mississippi John Hurt, Doc Watson and many other great blues and country players of the past and present.

To get your hands (and your brain) used to playing two musical lines, try this arrangement of *A' Soalin'*. The idea here is to separate the picking hand's role into two parts, much like the two hands of a piano player. Learn each part separately and then combine them. In the TAB, the thumb part is stemmed down and the finger part is stemmed up. Pay attention to the fingering of the left hand and the use of the right-hand fingers. No regular chord positions are used, only combinations of two notes at a time with some open strings in between.

Notice that the time signature is $\frac{2}{4}$. This means that there are two beats in each measure, with a quarter note equaling one beat. Count "1 & 2 &."

Traditional

M.M. = *88*

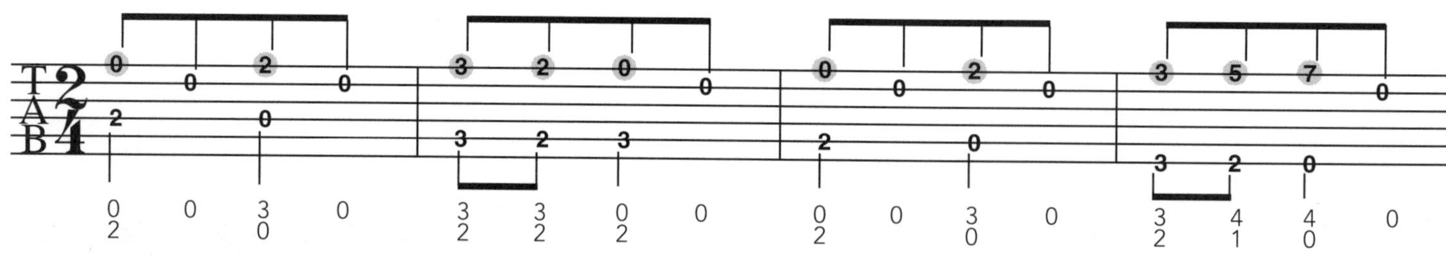

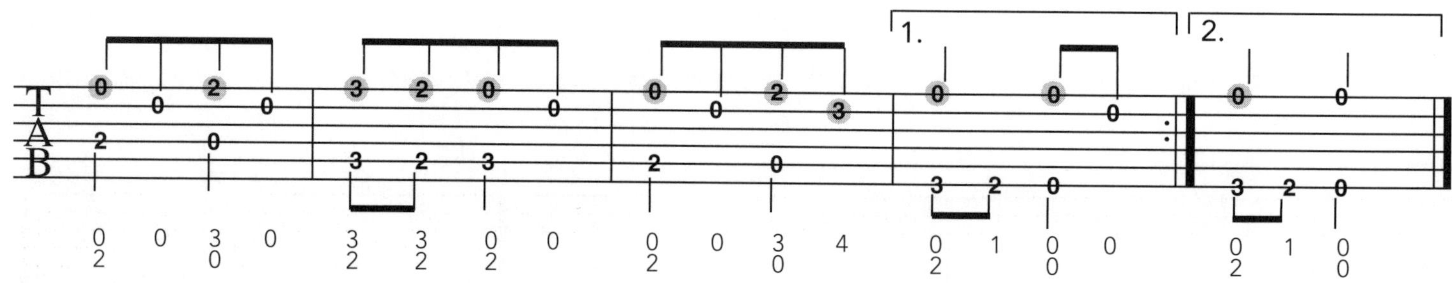

The next step is to let the thumb take over the basic rhythm that we have been using in our bass-chord playing. The *i* and *m* fingers will be used to pick the melody over this steady bass rhythm. To get the idea, use your thumb to play a steady rhythm under chords you know well.

Every chord in Example 36 has a standard two- or three-string pattern that the thumb can use to lay down the basic beat. Use your thumb to fret the low F on the F chord. This frees up fingers to fret melody notes later.

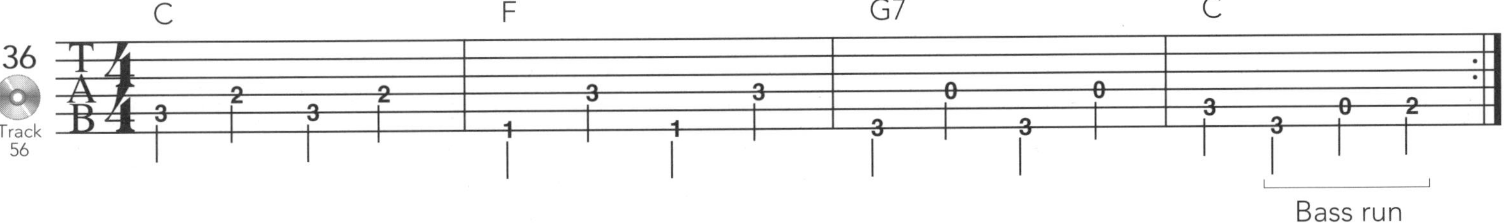

Use your thumb again to fret the low F♯ on the D7/F♯ chord. The letter after the slash refers to a bass note other than the normal root that is used.

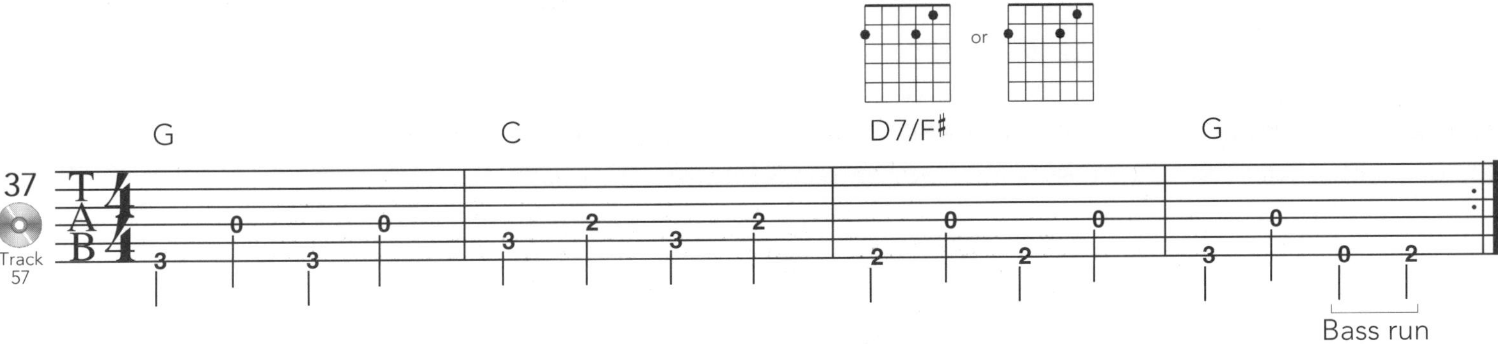

PHOTO • COURTESY OF STAR FILE, INC.

Ani DiFranco
started out as a solo folk singer in the 1980s. Her tireless non-stop touring and her founding of a very successful independent record label, make her one of the most popular folk performers on the contemporary scene.

Now it's time to try an arrangement with a steady thumb bass and a high string melody. I've chosen *Skip to My Lou* as our first tune because it is an easy melody to play. Use your ***m*** finger for the 1st string notes and your ***i*** finger for the 2nd string notes. After you have mastered that, use ***m*** for the 2nd string notes and ***i*** for the 3rd string notes. Learn the bass part first, then get the bass rhythm going on a C chord and add the high part. Go slowly at first and keep good time. As before, gray notes are the melody.

Skip To My Lou Solo

Track 58

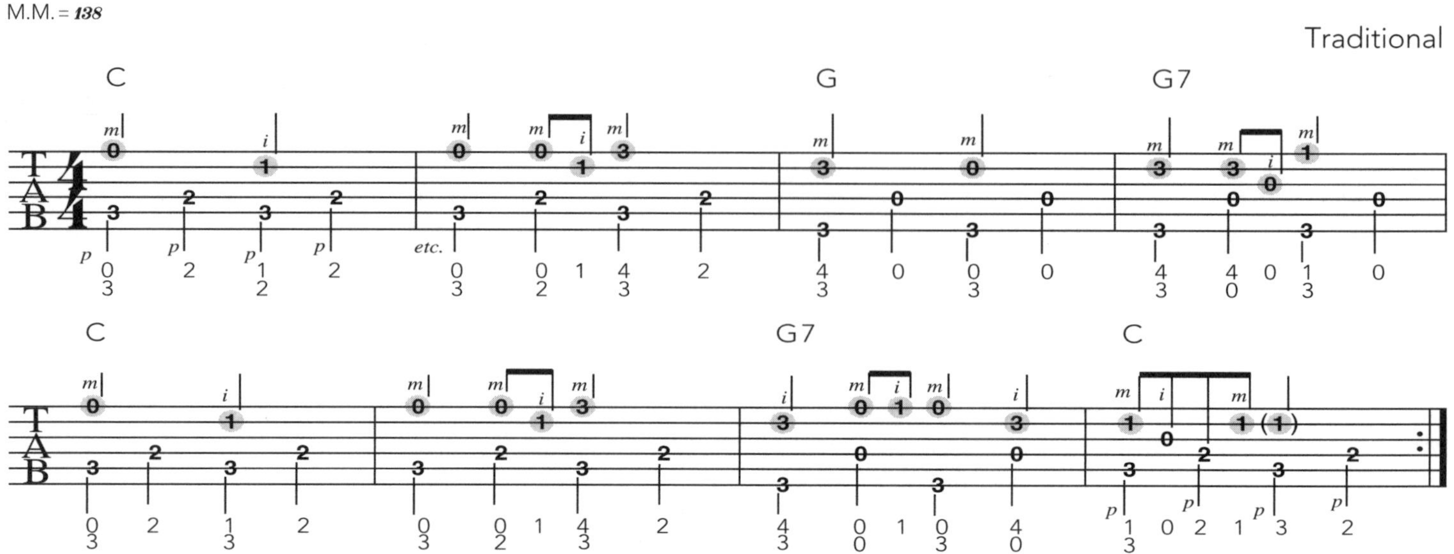

Notice that in *Skip to My Lou* Solo most of the melody notes are on the same beats as the bass notes but in the last measure a melody note falls between the bass notes. As you get better at this style you will be able to place melody notes on or off the beats as you like; that is, with or between the bass notes. This creates syncopation and more rhythmic interest.

PHOTO • COURTESY OF STAR FILE, INC.

Woody Guthrie

The legendary American folk singer is shown here with Margaret "Honey Chile" Johnson in a 1940 CBS radio show. He wrote many classic songs, such as This Land is Your land. *He was a major influence on Bob Dylan.*

In this arrangement of *Railroad Bill*, the melody is much more syncopated. Learn the bass part first and then add the melody. Use your thumb on the F chord (see the fingerstyle F chord on page 22) and your 4th finger to fret the 3rd fret notes on the 1st or 2nd string.

Railroad Bill

Track 59

M.M. = 160

Traditional

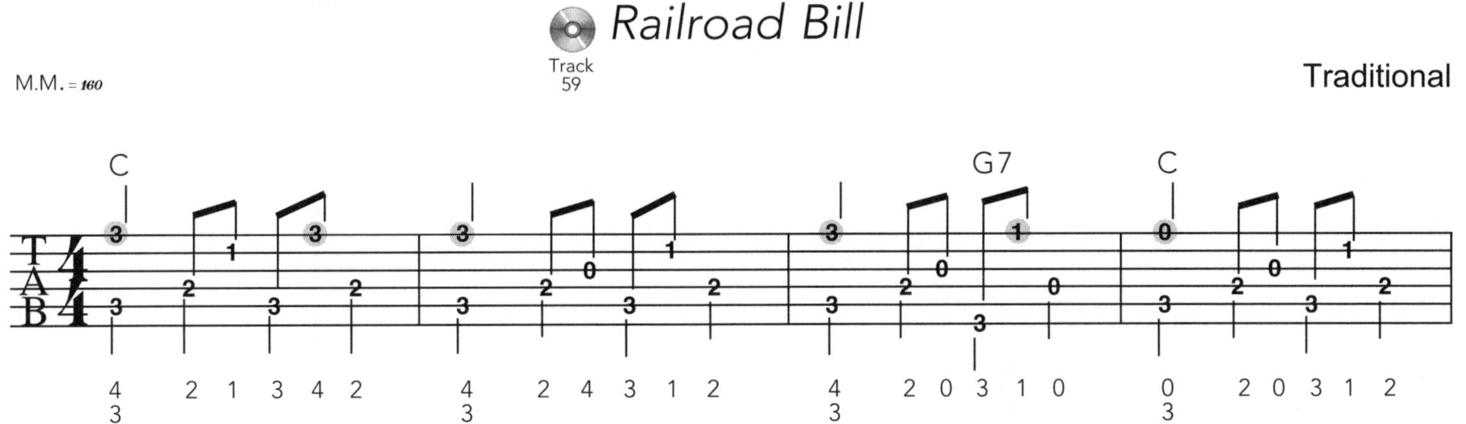

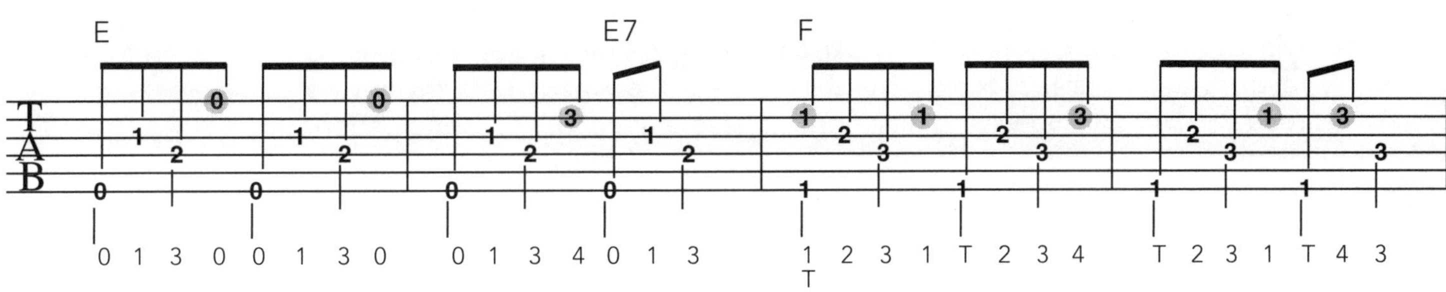

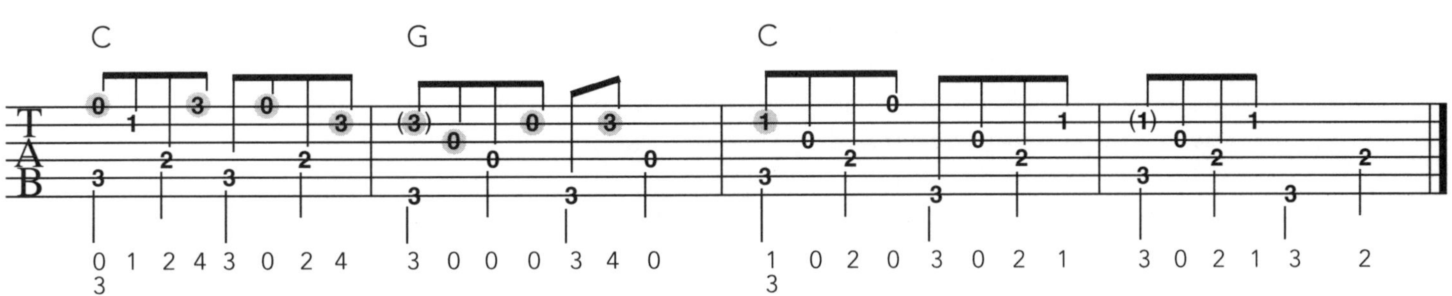

Drop D Tuning

Our last stop on this journey through the world of folk guitar is an alternate tuning. Guitars can be tuned in many different ways besides standard tuning. Most of these alternate tunings are called "open tunings" because the strings are tuned to an open chord. These tunings can create a beautiful, ringing sound. Of course, because the relationship from string to string is changed, all the chord fingerings change too.

We will examine one alternate tuning in this book. It is not an open tuning because only one string is changed from its standard pitch and there is no open chord. We will tune the 6th string down one whole step to D. To retune your guitar, compare the open 5th string to the 7th fret on the lowered 6th string for tuning purposes. If you have the optional CD for this book, you can tune to it (track 60). This tuning is called *Drop D tuning* and is especially nice for songs in the key of D since you now have a good low D note on the 6th string to use in your chords.

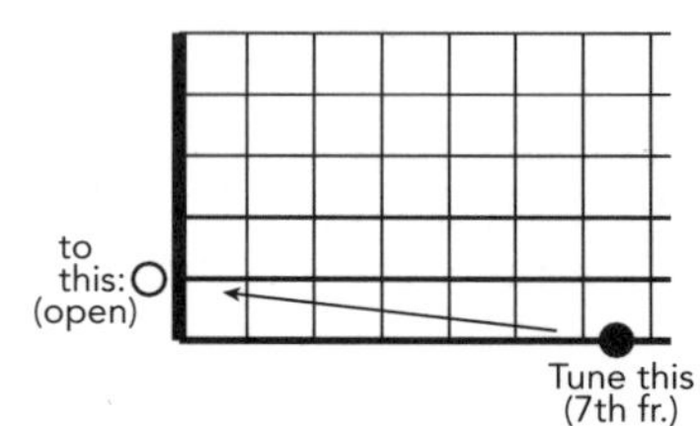

See the diagrams below for some basic chord fingerings in this tuning. Only notes that fall on the 6th string need to be re-fretted from their normal position. Notice there are a few nice ways to get a D chord by moving three-note chords up the neck on the first three strings. The three low strings can remain open, as they are all part of a D chord in this tuning.

The fingerstyle arrangement of *Fair and Tender Ladies* on the next page uses what is commonly referred to as *Travis picking*. The thumb plays the steady bass rhythm we used in *Railroad Bill*, and the fingers add high notes to create a repeating, rolling pattern with some variation. Two of these chords are played above the first five frets on the neck, so you will find "fr" markings identifying which frets the chords are on. (See page 7.)

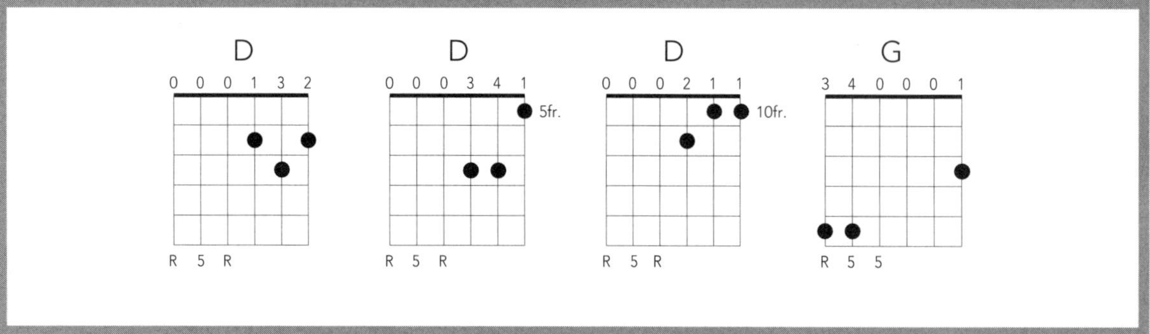

Watch out for the move in the A7 measure. It uses three two-note positions moving down from the 5th fret toward the 2nd fret. See the diagram below labeled A7 riff. In this riff, the fingers should go back and forth between the three circled groups of notes. The groups can be played in any order. Try starting on the 2nd fret and moving up to the 5th, then reverse the order.

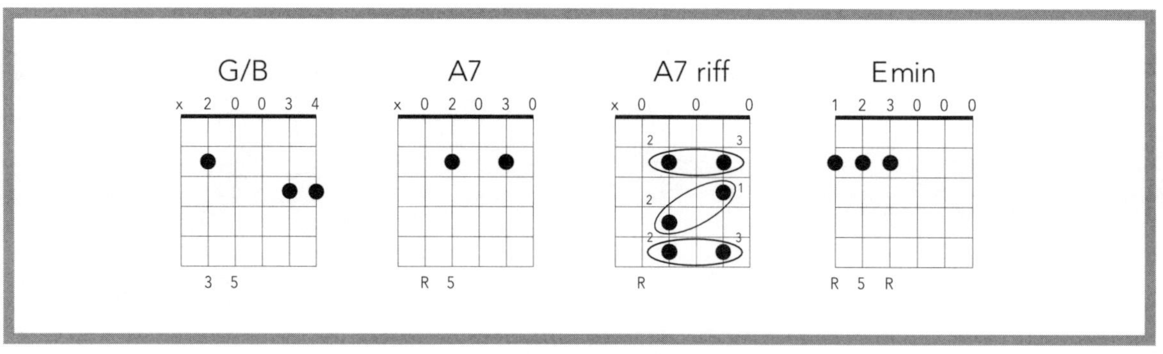

Fair and Tender Ladies
Track 60
Drop D Tuning
M.M. = 144
Traditional
1. Come all ye Fair and Ten - der La- dies. Take warn- ing
how you court your man. They're like a
star on a sum - mer morn - ing They first ap -
pear and then they're gone. 2. They'll tell to
D
A7
Emin
G
H
1.
2.
Let notes ring

How to Read Music

Pitch

Learning to read music will help you to get the most out of your National Guitar Workshop and Alfred instructional books. It will make you a better musician, too, because you will be able to communicate more easily with other musicians. What follows is a discussion of music reading basics. Remember that practice makes perfect! The more you practice reading, the easier it will become.

Staff

A staff containing five lines and four spaces is used in the writing of music. Notes are alternately written on the lines and spaces in alphabetical order.

Clef

The clef indicates which notes coincide with a particular line or space. Different clefs are used for different instruments. Guitar music is written in G clef. The inside curl of the G clef encircles the line which will be called "G." When the G clef is placed on the second line, as in guitar music, it is called the treble clef.

Using the G clef the notes are as follows:*

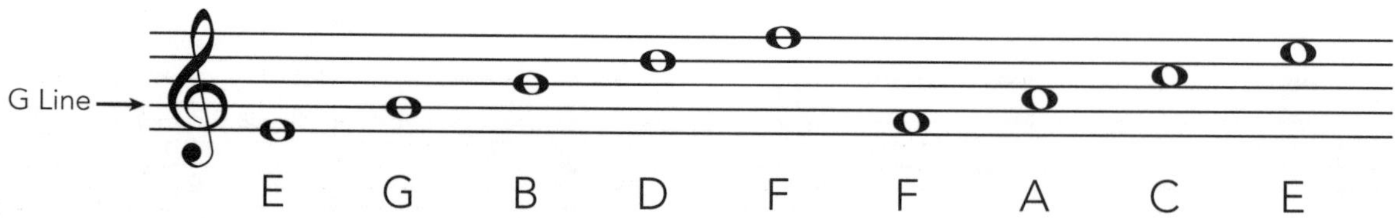

Ledger Lines

Ledger lines are lines that are used to indicate pitch above and below the staff.

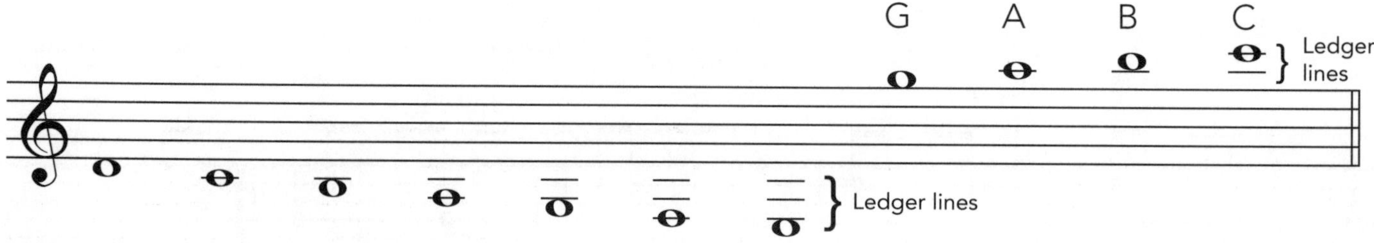

* In standard notation the guitar sounds an octave lower than written.

Time

The Measure

The staff is divided by vertical lines called bar lines. The space between two bar lines is a measure. Each measure (bar) is an equal unit of time.

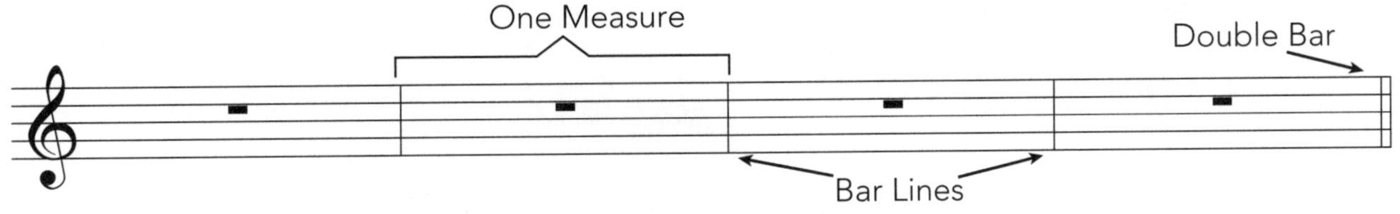

A double bar (𝄂) marks the end of a section or example.

Time Signature

Every piece of music has numbers at the beginning that tell us how to count the time.

Examples: 4/4 3/4 6/8

The top number represents the number of beats or counts per measure.

The bottom number represents the type of note receiving one count.
Example: 4 = quarter note 8 = eighth note

Sometimes a **C** is written in place of 4/4 time. This is called *common time.*

Note & Rest Values in Common Time

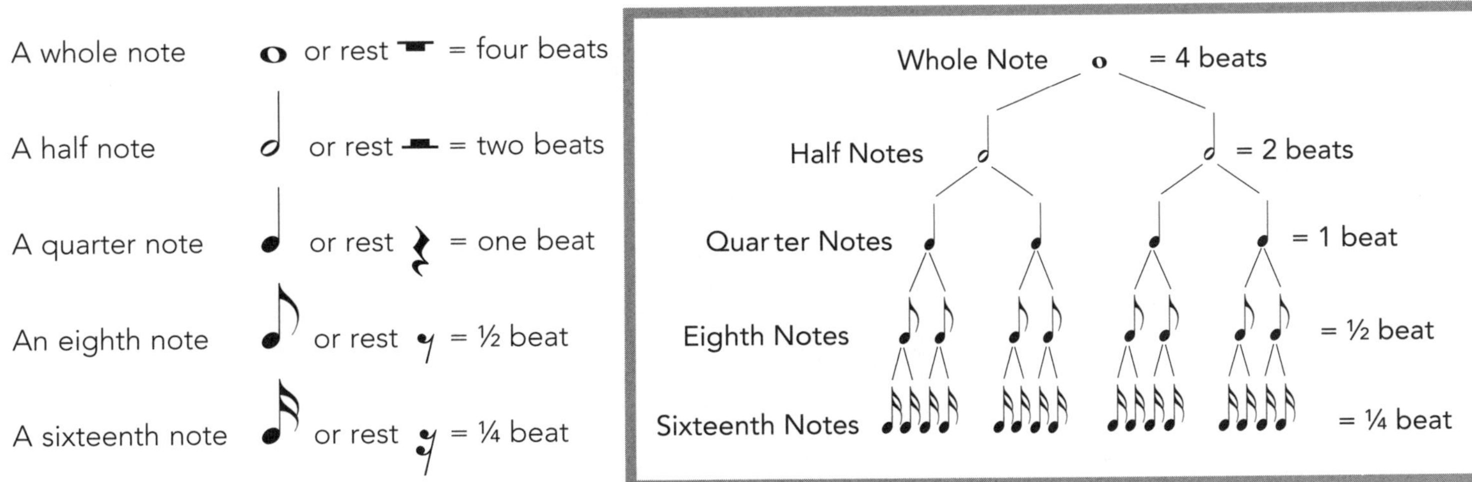

Notes shorter than a quarter note are usually beamed together in groups.

The Octava Sign 8va

8va means to play or sing one *octave* higher than written. An octave is the distance of one note to its nearest note of the same name.

IF YOU ENJOYED THIS BOOK, YOU'LL LOVE OUR SCHOOL!

NATIONAL GUITAR SUMMER WORKSHOP

- Study music in an intensive and friendly environment.
- Locations in Connecticut, California, Canada, Orlando, Austin, and Nashville.
- Students of all ages and levels enjoy learning from visiting artists and an outstanding professional faculty in week-long summer sessions.
- Classes are available for the beginner through the professional player.
- Design a course of study that fits your needs.

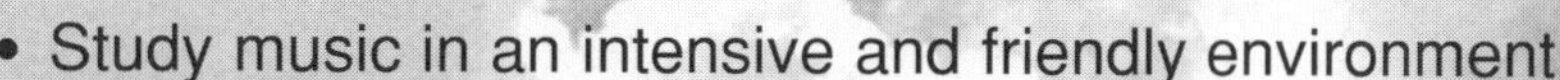

ROCK-BLUES-JAZZ-CLASSICAL
ACOUSTIC-COUNTRY-FUNK-FUSION
ALTERNATIVE-BASS-GUITAR-REPAIR
KEYBOARDS-SONGWRITING-DRUMS-VOICE

n.g.s.w

BOX 222
LAKESIDE, CT., 06758
1-800-234-6479

CALL OR WRITE FOR YOUR FREE BROCHURE